EILEEN GEORGE'S

CONVERSATIONS IN HEAVEN

AND PROPHETIC MESSAGES

AT A TIME SO NEEDED

Dialogues with Jesus and God the Father
COMPANION VOLUME TO
EILEEN GEORGE:BEACON OF GOD'S LOVE:HER TEACHING

THE MEET-THE-FATHER MINISTRY, Inc.
Millbury, Massachusetts

Grateful acknowledgments are made for permission to quote from:

The New Jerome Biblical Commentary, Brown/Fitzmeyer/Murphy, 1990, pp. 186-187, 199-200. Prentice Hall, Englewood Cliffs, NJ
Documents of Vatican II, Austin Flannery, O.P. Editor, new revised edition, 1992, Costello Publishing Co., Inc. Northport, NY
The New Jerusalem Bible, (c) 1985, Darton, Longman & Todd, Ltd. and Doubleday, a division of Bantam Doubleday Dell Publishing Group, Inc.
The Great Reckoning. How The World Will Change in the Depression of the 1990s, by James Dale Davidson and Lord William Rees-Mogg, 1991, Simon & Schuster, NY

Library of Congress Catalog Card Number: 92-85499
ISBN: 09624588-2-1
Imprimatur: Bishop Timothy J. Harrington, D.D.
July 15, 1992

The Imprimatur of the Bishop is not a judgment that the contents of a book are of supernatural origin, nor that it is free from error. It does indicate that the book contains nothing contrary to Catholic faith or morals.

This book is dedicated to the best of fathers,
God the Father,
that He may be better known and loved,
by you, the reader, and by all.

TABLE OF CONTENTS

PART FOUR: THE ROYAL PRIESTHOOD

PART FIVE: THE VALLEY

PHOTOGRAPHS

After FOREWORD

1. Bishop Timothy J. Harrington blessing Eileen at her service

2. Bishop Bernard Flanagan introducing Eileen

After INTRODUCTION

3. Bishop Daniel Reilly of Norwich, Conn. and Eileen at one of her Priest Retreats

4. Bishop Willem Michel Ellis, in whose diocese the Catholic Charismatic Conference was held at Aruba, Dutch West Indies in April 1992. Eileen was the principal speaker.

After PART TWO

5. Archbishop George Pearce, SM receiving renewed promises of priests at a Priests Retreat given by Eileen in September 1991

6. Monsignor Joseph Pepe, Chancellor of Archdiocese of Philadelphia, with Eileen

After PART FOUR

7. Monsignor Hugh Nolan, Ph.D., editor of the U.S. Bishops Pastoral Letters, and Eileen

8. Eileen with her private chaplain, Father Augustine Esposito, OSA

9. Father Norbert Weber, Pastor of Holy Family Church, Nazareth, Penn., and Eileen, March 1992

10. Eileen with diocesan priests to whom she has given a conference, Watertown, N.Y., June 1992

11. Eileen with Augustinian Priests after a Priests Conference, St. Mary's Church, Lawrence, Mass

12. Franciscan Seminarians with Eileen and Father Augustine Esposito, OSA

FOREWORD: PERCEPTIONS OF EILEEN GEORGE AND OF HER MINISTRY

The following perceptions taken from the book *EILEEN GEORGE: BEACON OF GOD'S LOVE:HER TEACHING*, Chapter One, are not an endorsement of the present book, rather they are an appreciation of Eileen and of her public ministry.

THE BISHOPS OF WORCESTER

Bishop Timothy J. Harrington introducing Eileen (Bishop Harrington has known Eileen for more than eighteen years.)

"Tonight we are the witnesses of the power of Christ Himself, pouring out from a woman gifted by Almighty God. That power will, if things happen as usual, most certainly send many away internally at peace and healed, and others healed right in this very spot, and others healed on the way home, or perhaps God willing, by Christmas day.

"Nevertheless, healed or not healed, we go away from a person like Eileen knowing God loves us, no matter how frail and weak and fragile we may be... What am I going to say about her that you have not heard? What can I add, except that in my mind she is a faith-filled, loving person and no matter how dreary the day or dark the night she is a person of hope. I say a person singularly blessed by Almighty God. And Eileen will say fast: I am not worthy, I am not worthy. No one of us merits those gifts of faith, hope and charity, nobody earns them, nobody deserves them, they are freely given gifts of God the Father, of the God she calls Daddy, of the Son, and of the Spirit in whose power she relies.

"So tonight as you pray for yourselves, pray also for the one here most in need, pray for all the others here, pray especially for

Eileen George, because she has been given much, and as Scripture says of those who have been given much, much is to be expected. May she not be found wanting in her return of her giftedness to Almighty God."

Bishop Bernard Flanagan introducing Eileen:

"It's a real pleasure for me to join with Eileen and with you who gather here for this service of teaching and healing. For many long years I have been aware of the many special gifts with which the Lord has blessed Eileen. So when the ministry called now Meet-The-Father was presented to me during my time as Bishop of Worcester, I was pleased to approve it, feeling very strongly that it would be a means of bringing a lot of our people closer to the Lord Jesus. And, after all, that is what we are all about in our ministry as priests and bishops, to help the people that we are assigned to serve to draw closer to the Lord Jesus. And I am sure that over the months, through these services that have been held here at St. John's Church, many of our people have felt closer to, and have been brought closer to, the Lord Jesus.

"You are all aware of that beautiful chapter in St. Paul's first letter to the Corinthians, the twelfth chapter, in which he writes about the gifts of the Spirit. And he goes on to say that although there is but one Spirit, nevertheless He distributes His gifts to each individual in different ways. And he mentions some of them: prophecy, healing, the utterance of wisdom, the utterance of knowledge, the gift of tongues, and the interpretation of tongues. But all these, he says, are the gifts of the one Spirit, and they are given to each of us for the common good.

"I think all of us are very much in debt to Eileen for being willing to share the gifts of the Lord to her, to share insights through her teaching, and in many cases her healings, to bring about a greater love of God in the hearts of so many people, and above all, that gift that I mentioned, bringing you closer to the Lord Jesus."

OTHER BISHOPS

Bishop Howard J. Hubbard of Albany: "I have heard many fine and positive things about Eileen's work and I believe that it is a blessing for our diocese to have her come to minister among our own people."

Bishop Robert E. Mulvee of Wilmington: "Bishop Harrington is a friend of many years. He speaks glowingly of you and your healing ministry and you have my permission to be present here in July."

Bishop Thomas J. Welsh of Allentown: "It will indeed be a grace for us to have her here again. Please assure her and the Bishop and her Director that she is most welcome."

John Cardinal O'Connor : "Please assure Bishop Harrington that the Cardinal has been informed of your work, and supports Monsignor Gartland in his intention to bring your special ministry to the parishioners of St. Patrick's [Bedford Village]."

Bishop Joseph F. Maguire : "Please know that you have a welcome from me to the Diocese of Springfield. I wish to state in this letter that it will not be necessary for you to request individual permissions. This letter in itself is indication that you are welcome here."

Bishop James C. Timlin of Scranton: "I hope that you will be able to come and I want to thank you in advance for whatever you can do to help deepen the faith of our good people."

Bishop Thomas Tschoepe of Dallas: "I have heard from Bishop Harrington, Bishop of Worcester, and he has highly praised the work that you are doing in this area of ministry. We will be most happy to have you here in the Diocese of Dallas."

Bishop Daniel P. Reilly of Norwich: "I join with Eileen in prayer that the Spirit may enrich with His gifts all who share in this Day of Healing."

Bishop Louis E. Gelineau of Providence: "I am aware of the great work you are doing in the Diocese of Worcester through the 'Meet The Father Ministry.' I appreciate your willingness to share your talents and gifts with the parishioners of St. Peter's parish."

Archbishop Theodore E. McCarrick of Newark: "She has the highest recommendation from my Coordinator for Charismatic Renewal. I look forward to meeting her."

Archbishop Roger Mahony of Los Angeles: "We at SCRC did check your credentials some time ago, including viewing a video tape of one of your healing services. We are satisfied that your ministry is authentic, Catholic and under proper submission to established Church authority... Archbishop Roger Mahony has asked that this letter be his own permission for your ministry here."

OTHERS

Father Joseph Pelletier introducing Eileen's first service at St. John's church, Worcester, October 24, 1982: "I've had a real sense of expectancy, the Lord is going to do some wonderful things here this afternoon... before you go home you will be saying, the Lord has done great things for us, we are filled with joy..."
God is a father to us all. Eileen's ministry is called Meet-The-Father . She is starting something new here ...."
"...I'd like you to know that she has had a preaching ministry for a long time. She has beautiful gifts from the Lord, three of her remarkable gifts are her inspired teaching, her prophetic ministry — she has been giving beautiful prophecies to our prayer group —

and the word of knowledge, which is a revelation from the Lord of healings that are taking place. She will use that gift here tonight. "Though there will be some physical healings here, I am sure the healing we need most and that Jesus wants for us most is spiritual healing, healing of our spiritual sight, and there is no day greater than ours when our faith is so menaced, more weakened by so many things. Our faith needs to be strengthened, and I am sure that the Lord wants to do that for all of us..."

Catholic Standard and Times, the Philadelphia Archdiocesan newspaper, about the Charismatic Rally Weekend presided over by Cardinal Krol, October 2, 1986: "Among the highlights were the faith-inspiring healing services and talks given by Eileen George, the nationally known charismatic speaker. In a personable but compelling way, she asked the people to 'praise and adore God. In this praise and worship, He will fill us with His love and healing power...by the time you leave on Sunday, you will know that God the loving Father has truly visited His people.' "

Monsignor Hugh J. Nolan, Ph. D. in the *Catholic Standard and Times*: "Nearly 200 persons from along the eastern coast under the guidance of the famed Eileen George have completed a five day retreat (July 10-14, 1989), at St. Joseph's-in-the-Hills, in Malvern.

"Mrs. George, who has spoken throughout the world, and who has been invited to China, had just finished conducting a retreat at Anna Maria College and opened the next evening at Malvern.

"Her retreat had been sold out for over four months. Of course, she will go nowhere without the permission of the local bishop, in this case Archbishop Bevilacqua, who was so favorably impressed by her last month at the Charismatic Rally in Villanova, under the able guidance of Msgr. Vincent Walsh , that the Archbishop knelt and received Eileen's prayer over him.

"She teaches most effectively the way to the Father, the way to solid sanctity stressing Penance and the Eucharist and the indispensable need for prayer. 'Love is what is needed. If you have the fullness of the Spirit, then you have the fullness of love for everyone.' "

Msgr. Vincent Walsh of the Archdiocese of Philadelphia, formerly Vicar of Tribunals and of Prayer Groups: "Once again, the priests at the Philadelphia Conference deeply appreciated Eileen's ministry. An overwhelming majority of the 135 priest participants found time during the retreat to go to her for personal ministry and prayer. At the end of the retreat, many many priests stated that it was the finest retreat that they ever made. This was due to Eileen's ministry as well as to the ministry of the other members of the team.

"For the Youth Weekend, the 155 young adults enjoyed her teachings and the results of the Young Adult Weekend were tremendous."

Father John Wallace, S.M. introducing Eileen: "You come here to see Eileen, to be with her and to be touched by her, but, above all, to pray with her, to praise the Lord and to thank Him for His constant love. I know that her great intention is to lead us to the Lord and to prayer to the Lord Jesus every moment of every day. I'd come to hear the Pope, any bishop, any priest, or any lay man or woman who is going to make prayer to the Father through the Lord Jesus in the Holy Spirit more important, precious and valuable.

"Whatever else you have on your mind, whatever healing you seek from the Lord, above all seek this gift, to spend the rest of the month in the presence of the Lord Jesus, until we see her again."

Father Chester J. Devlin, Principal of Marianhill High School, Southbridge introducing Eileen: "In the Gospel of Matthew we hear Jesus tell us that if we ask we shall receive... I think that when we rest our faith on the words of Jesus and... we make them a part of ourselves, then Jesus is welcomed into our lives and He really does great things for us.

"Last August I was sick and I came to see Eileen and I asked her if she would pray with me, and she did. And during the prayer she said to me: 'The Lord will heal you.' And two days later when I went to the doctor, the doctor said to me, 'Well Father that's what I call a miracle!' And so we give thanks to God for the wonderful gift that Eileen has been given to share with each of us.

"We know that God has really blessed Eileen George with a wondrous gift, with many gifts, and we ask her now to come and share these gifts with each of us so that we may give God glory and praise and thanksgiving."

Father Eugene Harrington, S.J. of Holy Cross College: "I think you'll agree with me on this, that love is like a fire which expands the hearts of men and women. That love is like a fire that inspires men to do heroic deeds. Like a fire, love wishes to spread itself everywhere, and change everything it touches into itself. Love engenders love. This is a good picture of the love of God for us....This is the love that drove Jesus to the cross on Calvary, there on the cross to extend His arms to embrace in love all mankind, everybody, you and me as well... and Mary's heart was united with His in His suffering and also in His love for each one of us...

"I think this is the love I see, and you see, in our sister Eileen George. Her love for God expands her heart so that it includes everyone. It includes those within the Church and those outside the Church, those in this country and in foreign lands, no matter what the race and creed—her love embraces all. Yet in her heart there is above all the desire that you and I may come to know and realize the love of God for each and every one of us. She wants us to come into an intimate and personal loving relationship with God the Father, in particular, and His Son Jesus Christ. In all her services the Father has blessed us abundantly with all His graces and, for some, even physical cures ... May the love of God the Father open our hearts, expand them, to receive the message He wishes to give through Eileen—and also the grace to inflame our hearts with love for Him. And so I call now on a true handmaiden of the Lord, Eileen George."

Mother Mary Clare, O.S.B., Prioress, St. Scholastica's Priory, Petersham, Mass, in the *Benedictine Bulletin:* "Just as the Church has fostered certain missions which have sprung from within her according to the needs of the time (under God always but also mediated through the Magisterium), it should not surprise us that God Himself throughout the ages has also given directly to others certain missions for the good of the Church, which the Church not only receives but also, as Hans Urs von Balthasar says, embodies their messages, 'imploring God in the universal holiness of the Church to send more such divine messengers.'

"It seems that today, in Worcester, God has yet again singled out such a messenger to show us how to live the Gospel of love in today's world. She is Eileen George, a wife and mother with eight children. Her message is simple: God wants everyone to realize He is a loving Father to His children on earth; He is caring, tender, gentle. He wants everyone to know of His great love for them; He wants a new world of peace, justice, and love; all who help bring this about will be blessed...

"Eileen has an aura of joy and love, and something wonderful, inconceivably beautiful about her. She loves her vocation of wife and mother... Eileen is a living witness and expression of the Church's tradition...

"And we know that through faith, one reaches a higher and deeper relationship with God than through visions and revelations. But when the latter are given for the good of others and the Church, it would be unfortunate to let negative safeguards be normative when such safeguards are not called for. Certainly Eileen is an affirmation that prayers are answered by God..."

"Simple, direct and unassuming as the salt of the earth, Eileen George is a light sent by God to a world that needs yet again to be made aware of His Love."

The National Catholic Register: "Throughout salvation history the Lord has chosen the most ordinary people to reveal His power, love and truth to the world. King David was a mere shepherd boy; Mary, a devout young girl from a small village; the Apostles, twelve unexceptional and uneducated men.

"Modern times are no different. The Lord continues to raise up common men and women to manifest His glory. One of these is Eileen George, a middle-aged housewife, mother of eight children and a cancer patient.

"In 1980 George was diagnosed as having malignant melanoma cancer of the regional lymph nodes. She was given six months to live and suffered through four surgeries. The disease is now in remission....

"Though her presence conveys saintliness, her human warmth and sense of humor would make any sinner feel welcome... Her healthy balance of the human and the divine is a living testimony of what it means to be a Catholic."
(From a four column article starting on the first page, June 16, 1985, titled: Mrs. George's Extraordinary Ministry .)

A Priest Retreatant : "Eileen, I am now closer to God than ever...
"Your relationship to Jesus is beautiful! Sharing your relationship to God with us inspired me to relate to Him on a personal-loving-tender level. For this I will always be indebted. This retreat was the best retreat I ever made... I have gotten new life from God... I am more aware of God's loving presence throughout my day. Scripture and prayer are no longer dry, but exhilarating!"

Eileen's Spiritual Director : "Eileen knows Heaven as we know earth!" (From a two page article about Eileen in the *Worcester Catholic Free Press*).

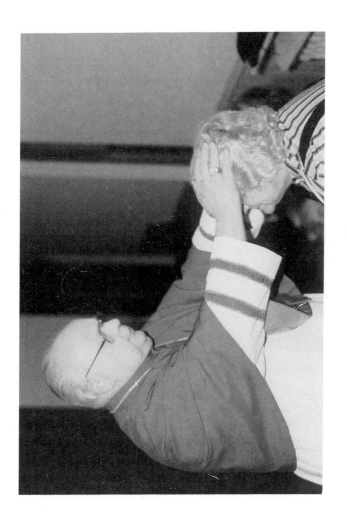

1. Bishop Timothy J. Harrington blessing Eileen at her service

2. Bishop Bernard Flanagan introducing Eileen

INTRODUCTION
WHAT YOU SHOULD KNOW
ABOUT THIS BOOK

I. ABOUT REVELATION

This is a book of revelations and prophecy. Many people do not accept prophecy, revelation or the supernatural. For them, everything has a natural explanation. Others see prophecy and revelation everywhere. The Church is cautious in this matter, but she knows that there are true prophets as well as false prophets.

In 1982 the Father showed Eileen events which were to begin in the 1990s. Eileen did not ask to know these things and was reluctant to hear them. She not only heard them, she witnessed them. Eileen has never divulged nor alluded to these events in the ten years of her public ministry. They are being made known now by her spiritual director, who recorded them at the time.

However, these prophecies are not the principal subject of this book. What is of more far reaching importance is the fact that these events were made known to Eileen in the place she will occupy in Heaven, if she remains faithful. This place Eileen describes in detail. She visits other "plateaus of Heaven," including one reserved to angels, and the highest where Mary embraces her.

These revelations make Heaven and the Persons whose companionship she enjoys there better known. We hear Eileen speaking with Jesus, with the Father, and with the Holy Spirit. At times they ask her to repeat what they are saying. Then we hear their words, which are intended for us. We are present at celebrations with the friends of Jesus and Eileen.

Outside of an authentic tradition, these are matters which are highly dubious and scary. Hence it is important to listen to what Scripture, the Church, and its experts, have to say about revelation and prophecy. Their teaching is coherent and clear. Then there is the question of Eileen George's credibility, which is discussed in *Eileen George:Beacon of God's Love:Her Teaching*, and which will be touched on here (see also the Foreword).

First of all, about public revelation, St. John of the Cross tells us that God the Father has given us all revelation in His Word, Jesus Christ. Hence, he holds that to look outside this Word for revelations is to dishonor the gift of God.[1] About public revelation *the Constitution on Divine Revelation* of Vatican Council II says, "He Himself (Jesus Christ) . . . completed and perfected revelation . . . and no new public revelation is to be expected before the glorious manifestation of our Lord Jesus Christ" [at the end of time]. (No 4)

Public revelation, completed and perfected in Jesus Christ, is the substance of Christian faith. It is all we need. St. John of the Cross advises us not to seek private revelations; those who desire the extraordinary are opening themselves to illusions. St. John of the Cross is concerned with directing souls to union with Jesus, and resting in the extraordinary is a detour on the road to this union.

There is a difference, however, between seeking the charismatic gifts for oneself, and seeking them for the upbuilding of the Church. To the Corinthians, who were "eager for spiritual powers," St. Paul said, "Aim to be rich in those that build up the community." And again, "Make love your aim; but be eager, too, for spiritual gifts, and especially for prophesying. Those who speak in a tongue speak to God . . . someone who prophesies speaks to other people, building them up, and giving them encouragement and reassurance . . . those who prophesy build up the community."[2]

Prophecy and revelation and other charisms need to be sifted and discerned by the Church, the pillar of truth.[3] Concerning the presence of the charismatic gifts in lay persons like Eileen, the Fathers of Vatican Council II in the *Constitution of the Church* tell us: "Christ is the great prophet . . . he fulfills this prophetic office not only by the hierarchy, . . . but also by the laity. He accordingly both establishes them as witnesses and provides them with the appreciation of faith (sensus fidei) and the grace of the word." (No. 35) *The Decree on the Apostolate of Lay People,* (No. 3), adds: "From the reception of these charisms, even the most ordinary ones, there arises for each of the faithful the right and duty of exercising them in the Church and in the world for the good of men and the development of the Church, of exercising them in the freedom of the Holy Spirit who 'breathes where he wills' (John 3:8), and at the same time in communion with his brothers in Christ, and with his pastors especially."

Furthermore, in the *Decree on the Ministry and Life of Priests,* (No. 9), the Council Fathers say: "While trying the spirits to see if they be of God, priests must discover with faith, recognize with joy, and foster with diligence the many and various charismatic gifts of the laity."

Thus the Church makes her own the teaching of St. Paul, who goes so far as to say that the Church is **built** on prophets and apostles. "You are built upon the foundations of the apostles and prophets, and Christ Jesus himself is the cornerstone."[4] He adds: "to some his (Christ's) 'gift' was that they should be apostles; to some prophets; to some evangelists; to some pastors and teachers to knit God's holy people together . . . to build up the Body of Christ . . . " (Ephesians 4:11)

Prophets are those God chooses as His messengers to bring the revelation He made once and for all in Christ to the attention of the Church. Karl Rahner writes of the prophet: "He is the envoy of God . . . He proclaims a message which makes demands . . . The prophet is the 'bearer of revelation'. . . . Jesus Christ is *the* great prophet, the absolute bringer of salvation. This does not mean that prophecy has simply ceased. But the only [true] prophets are those who strive to uphold his message in its purity, who attest that message and make it relevant to their day . . . charismatic prophecy in the Church helps to make the message of Jesus new, relevant and actual in each changing age."[5]

Prophecy then is a message from God. Father Bruce Vawter explains in a section of the *New Jerome Biblical Commentary* entitled, "The Nature of Prophecy": "By prophecy we understand not specifically or even principally the forecasting of the future . . . but rather the mediation and interpretation of the divine mind . . . Prophecy not only was, but still is, the word of God. If all Scripture is, in its own measure, the word of God, it is preeminently true of the prophecy in which God chose to speak directly with his people. It is . . . the living word of a living God . . . the prophetic word is power from God and the prophet is the instrument through which this word is transmitted."[6]

Father Vawter is speaking of prophecy in general as an introduction to the prophets of the Old Testament. However, he says that "true and false prophets abound not only in antiquity, in the Old Testament and New Testament, within and without the people of God, but also in later times . . . it is plain that God spoke to his people through such instruments as Francis of Assisi, Vincent Ferrer, Catherine of Siena, Bridget of Sweden, and others, often through experiences like those of the biblical prophets."[7]

Thus during the Jansenist heresy, a withering wind blowing through the Church and shriveling trust in the mercy of God, Christ gave St. Margaret Mary Alacoque (1647-1690) the revelation of His Sacred Heart. This revelation was made known by her spiritual director, Saint Claude de la Colombière, S.J., calling to the attention of all the mercy and love of Christ.

And in 1858, in the materialistic 19th century which no longer believed in miracles or Heaven, God sent His Mother to fourteen year old Bernadette to establish a shrine at Lourdes. Here a number of cures have been attested by an international commission of medical doctors (including agnostics), cures which cannot be explained by medical science.

Then God showed His concern for mankind through revelations to three children at Fatima, May to October 1917, when a wave of militant atheism was about to sweep the world and carry away a third of it. This wave of unbelief encouraged the already widespread rejection of the supernatural, nourishing seeds of doubt and atheism everywhere. It left in its wake a distorted and inhumane form of liberalism, which was imbibed by many of the intellectuals of the Church, and with them by many of the faithful. It is only recently that the devastation worked in the Communist countries has been clear for all to see.

Against this spirit of disbelief, God sent Our Lady to the children at Fatima to reveal forthcoming events, to reaffirm truths of faith and to establish devotion to her Immaculate Heart. God pointed to Mary's heart as a sure way to the Heart of His Son and to His own. To Mary He confided the peace of the world. The message of Our Lady of Fatima, the message of the Hebrew prophets and of the Gospel, repent and pray, was given to an age which has been losing its sense of sin and self-control.

II. ABOUT EILEEN

Is it inconceivable that God has raised up Eileen George, at a time so needed, when the Church is endangered and a divine chastisement hangs heavy on the world? Is it unreasonable to believe that He wishes to reveal the Father and His tender love and mercy at this time; to remind the world and priests that the way to the Father is through the love of Jesus; and that the way to the love of Jesus is through love of neighbor, fidelity to one's duties and through the sacraments of the Church? In our day the sacrament of Reconciliation has fallen into disuse in the Church, while Jesus' real presence and transforming action in the Eucharist has been pushed in the background. Today the family, too, is under attack.

The *Decree on the Apostolate of Lay People* of Vatican Council II tells us that the laity has a "special and indispensable role in the mission of the Church. Indeed, the Church can never be without the lay apostolate; it is something that derives from the layman's very vocation as a Christian." (No 1) Is it not fitting that the Father should choose as a preacher and example of His love a laywoman, wife and mother of eight; one especially devoted to the duties of her state of life; a model of family life; a woman devoted to prayer who generously accepts repeated trials and sufferings to obtain the graces of conversion and holiness for all and especially for priests?

Does not our tottering Western and world society need a powerful renewal? And who better than the Father can initiate it? For more than fifty years sociologists have been reminding us that we are in a **post-Christian** era.

A Harvard psychiatrist has noted that whereas previously the most common mental disorders were due to repression, now they are due to lack of impulse control. He sees this as a result of the weakness of the father in the family.[8] With the breakdown of the family, the development of the character of children is impaired. Hence they are a prey to sex, alcohol, drugs, incapacity to make commitments, violence, suicide, need for immediate gratification, and to the loss of control of their impulses. Children who have not suffered this impairment are subject nonetheless to the peer pressure of the others, who form the juvenile culture of today.

"A community that allows a large number of young men [*and women*] to grow up in broken families . . . never acquiring any stable relationship to male authority, never acquiring any set of rational expectations about the future . . . that community asks for and gets chaos" said Daniel Patrick Moynihan, sociologist, professor at Harvard and U.S. Senator.[9]

THE REMEDY: GOD THE FATHER

Knowledge of and devotion to God the Father is a remedy for the rapid deterioration of the family and society. The Father (whom Eileen says has all the solicitude and tenderness of a mother) is not withdrawing attention from Jesus, the Redeemer, nor from the Holy Spirit, the guide and lover of souls, nor from the signal importance of women. On the contrary the Father points to the love of Jesus as the way to His own heart and to awareness of the Holy Spirit. And He exalts the role of women by pointing to Mary as *the* Woman, the way to oneness with Jesus and with Himself, and by choosing a woman to be His confidante and messenger.

Crucial to the Church and the world today is the realization of the role of the Father and of the Trinity in human affairs and in the search for happiness. Walter Kasper, theologian and now Bishop, a successor to Karl Rahner, has come to the same conclusion. It is the theme of his book *The God of Jesus Christ.*[10]

Eileen's revelations are addressed to all. But they are meant in a special way for priests, on whom the welfare of the faithful and the world so much depends. Hence the editor has not suppressed what concerns priests. Eileen has a special devotion to the "royal priesthood of Jesus Christ" and has had a ministry to priests for more than thirty years. When she speaks to them she doesn't permit lay persons or even deacons to be present. She avoids criticism of priests. She constantly teaches lay persons to love their priests and not to judge them. She reminds people that Christ reserves the judgment of His priests to Himself. And this reflection is offered to the readers of this book.

The book *Eileen George:Beacon of God's Love:Her Teaching*[11] was published in 1990, eight years after Eileen's public ministry began. It presents her public teaching given in parish renewals, conferences, retreats, and in her publicly distributed meditative tapes. It also relates facts about her life, her mission and her credibility. And it shows how her mission is being accomplished in the power of the Spirit and in accord with the Scriptures and the teaching of the Church.

Conversations In Heaven, on the other hand, records dialogues between Eileen, Jesus and the Father. They could easily be dismissed as a mirage. Why indeed should these supposed quotations from God the Father be given any credence at all? Like the Gospels, these words can stand on their own, but their credibility has a solid basis. First, what is said of her mission is being fulfilled in fact in one of the fastest growing ministries in the Church. Second, people are brought closer to the Father by Eileen. Third, she leads a simple, unpretentious, eminently Christian life. She is fulfilled in a happy family life as a mother of eight and a housewife. All money received for her services goes not to her, but to the Meet-The-Father Ministry, a nonprofit organization. Having terminal cancer and many illnesses, her ministry is carried out at great personal sacrifice. Fourth, many healings take place through her ministry. "The works I do in my Father's name are my witness" (John 10:25).

Prophecy is proven by the occurrence of the foretold event. In this book we see foretold Eileen's far reaching mission, which has since taken place. At a time when Eileen is a member of a local prayer group, we see the Father assuring Eileen that she will give His teaching to many priests and people. She does not understand how she can reach priests, other than those who come to the prayer meeting. Since then, however, Eileen has been giving retreats to priests on an annual basis. She has also been retreat master together with Father Vincent Walsh [then vicar for charismatic groups and officialis of the Archdiocese of Philadelphia], and with others, to hundreds of priests. For years she held a weekly "Priests Day" attended by priests from several dioceses.

Eileen is responsive to the Father's instructions concerning her mission. Eileen was a homebody. When the Father reveals the use He will make of her we hear Eileen respond that she doesn't like to travel. She hopes He will use her near home. Since then she has been to Korea twice, to Canada, the Dutch West Indies, Rome and to various parts of the United States.

We hear Eileen being chided by the Father for not giving out in her prayer group the prophecies He gives her, because she does not want to center attention on herself. Since then Eileen has been a featured speaker before thousands at the Philadelphia Civic Center, in the Olympic Gymnastic Stadium in Seoul (before 30,000), and elsewhere. The Father says He will open the door and she must go through it. She asks Him not to open too many. Since then she has had a full schedule, despite the fact that she has melanoma of the lymph glands, a fatal fast growing cancer, diagnosed and operated on in 1980, with a prognosis of 6 months to 2 years of life. Her oncologist said that a young healthy woman would have trouble following her schedule.

So the Father's predictions and instructions regarding Eileen's mission made in 1982 and related in this book have been fulfilled in the intervening ten years.

Cardinals, bishops and priests have accepted Eileen's ministry in their (arch)dioceses and parishes. From the laity she has received ovations for her preaching, and more importantly, many have been led to the sacrament of Reconciliation. Indeed, at parish renewals there are often seven or more priests hearing confessions.

Eileen's hearers and readers recognize that she speaks from experience about the kingdom and about the persons of the Trinity. They wish to know more of her actual experiences—to go "behind the scenes." *Conversations In Heaven* takes them behind the scenes, showing how Jesus and the Father prepared Eileen for this teaching and healing mission. Thus these two books complement and confirm each other.

WHEN FAITH FALTERS

Believers need to cling firmly to public revelation, that is to Scripture and Tradition, and to its authentic interpretation by the living teaching office of the Church. This is the foundation of the believer's divine and Catholic faith.[12] It is by this that private revelation is to be judged and not vice versa. The value of private revelation, as Karl Rahner says, is that it can recall the Gospel message according to the needs of the time. It can enliven, renew and deepen faith when it is faltering and becoming confused. That is the purpose of this publication, but its fidelity to public revelation must be judged by the Church. The Imprimatur (that is, "let it be published") of the Bishop is not a judgment that the contents of a book are of supernatural origin, nor that it is free from error. But the Imprimatur does indicate that the book contains nothing contrary to Catholic faith or morals.

Take these dialogues as dreams, or as meditations, or if they ring true, as revelations, pending the judgment of the Church. What Eileen sees and experiences of the kingdom can excite in us a deeper faith, that our hearts and lives may be filled with the joy of the Messiah, that we may look forward more eagerly to the joys awaiting us in our heavenly home. Eileen's experiences become our experience. They draw us to love the divine Persons and to accept their unbounded love for us with simplicity.

Are these revelations about Heaven revealed for one group of people only? As all people are the beloved children of the Father, so the mysteries of His love are for all. The Father is close to, and working in, all who have unselfish love, even those who do not believe in God. Eileen says: "Love is indestructible. It is a sacred flame that burns forever. It comes from Heaven and to Heaven it returns. Those err who say that love can die." Some people may not know or acknowledge God, but He knows and loves them. These revelations then are for all who will accept them, to encourage all to come to the Father so that there may be in His Son one flock and one shepherd.[13]

The calamities that the world faces according to the prophecies recounted herein, a small part of this book, are not sent by the Father. They are the result of sin and of natural causes. He nevertheless can ordain them for the good of the human family. "All things work together for good for those who love God." Prayer may modify or alter these events and conversion to God may help persons to pass through them with divine protection and without spiritual loss.

IS HEAVEN AS EILEEN DESCRIBES IT CREDIBLE?

In our times, marked by an exalted sense of science and reason, we have been given empirical evidence of the survival of the soul and of its operation without the assistance of the body. In this life, the intellect depends upon the body, since to have a concept we need an image supplied by the brain. In the near death experience, when the person is clinically dead, and when the brain is no longer functioning, the person has a sense of well-being and wholeness, and the mind operates with much greater speed. Those not acquainted with this phenomena will find it described in *The After Death Experience. The Physics of the non-Physical*, by Ian Wilson, who received an honors degree in history from Magdalen College, Oxford in 1963. (New York: William Morrow and Company, Inc., 1987.)

The happiness of Heaven is essentially the face to face vision of the Father, the Son and the Holy Spirit. "But I in my uprightness will see your face, and when I awake I shall be filled with the vision of you" (Psalms 17:15). However, the resurrection of the body assures us that there is also the human happiness of interpersonal relations with those whom we love in Heaven. Moreover, the love of God's creation, which is present in Heaven, is not limited to the intercourse with others, human, or angelic.

God created beings in all possible divisions, though not exhausting the type of beings in these divisions. Thus there is material creation and immaterial creation, and the composite, which is the human being. In material creation, there are creatures without life, and with life. And of those with life there are those with sense and without sense. Hence there are earth, vegetation including flowers and fruits, animals, man and angels.

"Eye has not seen nor ear heard what God has prepared for those who love Him." Nevertheless it is not inconceivable that all grades of beings made by the Father in His Son and through the Holy Spirit, are present in Heaven. We expect a new earth and new heavens, and they may contain plants and animals, brooks, fields and mountains. "Then I saw *a new heaven and a new earth;* the first heaven and the first earth had disappeared now, and there was no longer any sea" (Rev. 21:1). "What we are waiting for, relying on his promises, is the new heavens and new earth, where uprightness will be at home" (2 Peter 3:13). "For we are well aware that when the tent that houses us on earth is folded up, there is a house for us from God, not made by human hands but everlasting, in the heavens" (2 Cor.5:1).

Moreover, while pets cannot merit Heaven, nor have they souls which endure after their death, yet the persons whom God loves may be given the pets they loved on earth by Him to whom all things are possible, and who does whatever will make His children happy.

But how does it stand with regard to human souls before the resurrection? Scripture tells us of corporeal appearances of angels, of Gabriel to Mary at the Annunciation, of the angels who appeared as men to whom Abraham gave hospitality, and of Raphael who conducted Tobias to his destination and back. We are advised by Scripture to extend hospitality to strangers, because our fathers in doing so entertained angels.

Angels, St. Thomas teaches, can by their own power fashion bodies by which they can appear to men (*Summa Theologiae* 1,51,2). They are not united to these bodies as our souls enliven our bodies. Their bodies are merely the instruments through which their angelic power expresses itself to us. God can fashion bodies for the souls in Heaven awaiting the resurrection. In this case also the bodies are not animated by souls as a body is animated by its soul in this life, but simply moved as an instrument. At the resurrection, however, our soul will be truly and substantially reunited to our body.

"In my Father's house there are many places to live in" (John 14:2), Jesus tells us. Are these places lined up in a row like houses on a street? Rather it seems to me that they are one above another, there where there is no law of gravity. St. John of the Cross tell us that in the evening of our life we will be judged by love alone.

Those with more love will have a higher degree, a higher place in Heaven, closer to the Trinity forever. All will be filled to the brim with happiness, but those whose love is greater will have a higher place. Eileen calls these plateaus. She says that those on a higher plateau will be able to come down to visit those on the lower ones, but those on the lower, having reached their limit, will not be able to visit the higher ones. She urges all to seek by the grace available to all the highest plateau!

These considerations, conformable to Scripture, reflect possibilities which are without inherent contradiction. And these considerations may allow those who may otherwise have difficulty with Eileen's experiences to receive them with an open mind, aware that with God all things are possible, and that His goodness and love surpass our comprehension.

While Eileen often wishes that people could know of Heaven and share in her experiences there, because of the good it would do their souls, she and Jesus realize the difficulty people will have in accepting the reality of these experiences. Nevertheless this is the revelation which the Father wishes to make known at this time, at a time when it is so needed, for those who are open to accept it.

"I bless you, Father, Lord of heaven and earth, for hiding these things from the learned and the clever and revealing them to little children" (Matt 11:25). The kingdom of God is already being built. It is not made with hands. It is this kingdom that the Father reveals to us in this book.

EILEEN REMAINS EILEEN

Eileen remains herself while responding to the persons of the Trinity. She adores, loves, argues, questions, jokes, and in the end, submits. Pert though she is, she refuses nothing that God asks of her. If Eileen is an independent and strong-willed person, above all, she has an abiding sense of her own nothingness, a dependence on grace, and gratitude for the least grace given her.

To a prophet the divine light is given to know things which should be told the people of God for the building up of the Church. (Hence the prophet's "private" revelation is not strictly private. We call it "private" to distinguish it from "public revelation," which ended with the apostles.) Even though the prophet's mind is raised to the consideration of divine things, he is not necessarily a friend of God.[14] "'Lord, Lord, did I not prophesy in your name.' Then I will declare to them: I never knew you."[15]

Eileen is not only a prophet. She is also a close friend and intimate of Jesus and the Father, the spouse of the one, the faithful loving daughter of the other. God cannot withhold revealing His secrets from His close friends. He is goodness itself. As St. Thomas says when explaining the reasons for the Incarnation, goodness desires to communicate itself.[16] Of Abraham God said, "Shall I conceal from Abraham what I am going to do?"[17] Of Moses: "Yahweh would talk to Moses face to face as a man talks to his friend."[18] Of David God said: "I took you from the pasture from following the sheep, to be leader of my people Israel; I have been with you wherever you went."[19] John leaned on the bosom of Jesus[20] and learned from Him His secrets.

At this time when the Father discloses to Eileen that His Church is in serious danger He speaks face to face with her. Where the prophet is in contact with God Himself, the source of the prophetic light, there is the highest degree of prophecy.[21] Because of the uniqueness of her mission, the Father gave Eileen His Son as a companion from her childhood, then as a spouse. It was to make Heaven known that he brought Eileen into his heavenly kingdom and revealed its secrets to her. Eileen knows Heaven as we know earth — from being there.

Humility, trust, generosity, willingness to embrace the sufferings of the cross, and obedience are necessary for friendship with God. Human qualities — education, intelligence, special natural gifts — do not qualify a person for the divine friendship. Indeed their absence makes it more clear that it is God who is living and working in His friend. Friendship with God is a matter of a mutual love, given, accepted and worked for perseveringly. Rare are they who could receive such divine favors as God has accorded Eileen without a secret pride which would alienate them from God, Who resists the proud, but inclines to the humble. Her Bishop, Bishop Harrington, has said that despite her ministry and her gifts, Eileen remains the unassuming person she has always been.

If the ardor of the exchanges of love between Jesus and Eileen surprises us, perhaps it is because we have not sufficiently appreciated these three little words of St. John: "God is love" (1 John 4:16). God's love is divine. It is infinite. It is incomprehensible to us in its extent and condescension.

In the love between Jesus and Eileen, you and I are never forgotten. While God gives His favors to whom He will, He does so for the welfare of others also. Eileen's humility and love entice us to enter into a closer friendship with the Father and Jesus. The love which Eileen pours out on the divine Persons, she also gives freely to others. She wishes all to have the benefit of her unique experiences.

Many can testify to Eileen's lavish self-sacrificing love. The Father's repeated instructions to her to withdraw into silence and solitude have proven a difficult cross for her. Compliance means not being available for one-to-one help to people. This goes against the grain of her deeply rooted compassionate desire to reach out to and help people in distress. The Father wants her now to reach out to them by prayer and sacrifice. He wants her to follow her deep attraction to the silence and solitude in which she can hear His voice, converse with Him and her beloved Jesus, receive His communications, and thus be better prepared to deliver His messages in her services.

Sequels to the present book, which will continue the conversations of Eileen with Jesus and the Father from September 1982 to 1987, will show how the Father persuaded Eileen to reveal some of her heavenly experiences in her public teaching. The Father

pointed out to Eileen the awe with which her audiences received
the hints of her heavenly experiences, and how their spiritual
appetites were awakened. Hence a foretaste of these revelations
are contained in the book of her public teaching: *Eileen George:
Beacon of God's Love:Her Teaching.* Ten years of Eileen's public
ministry throughout this country and abroad stand as a testimony
to the revelations of this present book.

Eileen does not speak with the tongue of human eloquence
but with simplicity and the charm of an honest personality
endowed with mature common sense, prudent judgment, and a
sense of humor. Her public teaching is supported not by argu-
ments of humanly perfected reasoning, but by the power of the
Holy Spirit and by the healings which accompany it.

Eileen is simply herself in these conversations, yet her
speech becomes lyrically beautiful at moments of intense love.
The Father and Jesus speak to Eileen in her terms and at her level
(which is also ours), showing the condescension of the Incarnation. Thus They assure us that They wish to enter into our lives,
and prayer, just as we are. Yet at moments They speak with
unsurpassed splendor.

Nevertheless, the charm of this book is in the tenderness of
these conversational partners. No attempt has been made to elim-
inate the playfulness of Jesus and Eileen, both of whom have
retained their childlike hearts, nor to disguise the humor of the
Father. These are a revelation in themselves and bring us closer to
the divine Persons. Eileen's mission is to bring us into a more
intimate union with Jesus Christ and the Father — and all their
children. By rereading this book, you will provide the opportunity
for her mission to be accomplished.

THE EXAMPLE OF EILEEN GEORGE — WHAT TO AVOID

The Father's message given through Eileen commends the
way of faith and love. Through faith we are united to Christ. By
meditation on the truths contained in our faith we assimilate His

message and put our life in order. Faith leads us to the sacraments of Reconciliation with its emphasis on amendment of life and to the Eucharist, by which we are intimately united to Jesus. Eileen did not choose the way she was led. It was only gradually that she realized this way was not for everyone, but was a privilege. Often Eileen wished that everyone could see Heaven as she does, as an incentive to becoming better people. Often she advises our Lord to show Himself to His priests that they may believe He is present in the Eucharist and in the tabernacle. Jesus denies that this will be the way to the conversion of priests or the world. He insists that it is by seeking a personal relationship with Himself in faith that conversion will come about. He points to the need for an ever increasing faith, a gift to be asked for, but also something that one must work for.

Priests and lay people are often attracted to the extraordinary in Eileen's life. They want to have a ministry like hers. They want to be in the forefront and attract the attention of crowds. Eileen moans that they do not know the price of such a ministry — the suffering, humiliations, persecutions that it brings, and through which it becomes fruitful.

Eileen urges priests and people to be faithful to the duties of their state of life. For priests this means accepting and being faithful to the ministry given them by their Bishop. She recommends awareness of the great privilege which is theirs to celebrate Mass and to hear confessions and give absolution. She commends the power of the Word, proclaimed in fidelity to the Scriptures, sound doctrine and tradition. She recommends obedience to the Church in its doctrine and discipline.

Nevertheless, Eileen is vividly aware of the value of the charismatic gifts, the graces *gratis datae,* poured out so profusely during the Charismatic Renewal, a movement which has elements of enduring value. She only insists that they be exercised in true selfless love for the welfare of the Church, in the Church, and under ecclesiastical obedience and supervision. The gifts for

which Eileen prays, in her novena to the Holy Spirit, are the
sanctifying gifts of the Holy Spirit, wisdom, understanding,
knowledge, counsel, fortitude, piety and fear of the Lord, without
which the charismatic gifts cannot be rightly exercised, nor exercised without harm to the person gifted with them. Christ taught
that he who wishes to be first should become the last and the
servant of all; that the exalted will be humbled and the humble
will be exalted.[22]

With regard to the Charismatic movement in the West,
Eileen, in agreement with the opinion of some U.S. leaders of this
movement, believes that its decline is associated with the pursuit
of the charismatic gifts without due subordination to "the best way
of all,"[23] the way of love — the pursuit of God Himself through
personal holiness. Charismatics, like all believers, need to pursue
the love of God in and through the means offered by the Church,
its sacraments, personal prayer which leads one into a deeper
personal encounter with Jesus, spiritual reading, the amendment
of their lives.[24]

The gist of the revelations given to Eileen for the world is the
recommendation of LOVE, as Christ teaches it. Love involves
reconciliation with people, the forgiveness of injuries and the
burial of grudges, it involves the service of others, not the service of
one's own importance.[25] The humble are those who are most
important to Jesus and to the Father.

These remarks may be helpful so that the revelations of God
to Eileen presented in this book may be fruitful. The gifts He has
given Eileen, and others like her, are given gratuitously by God to
whom He wills. But greater gifts are offered to all without excep-
tion — the gift of becoming the beloved and favored child of the
Father, and of becoming oneself—the wonderful person God has
made you to be, and wants you to become, your true self.

III. ABOUT THIS BOOK

THE SETTING

Eileen in October 1979 called a monastery to pose a question to a priest to whom the Father had directed her. It happened that this priest answered the phone and agreed to see her. He recognized that the graces she had received were in preparation for a special mission in the Church. When she again called and came to see him, he agreed to be her spiritual director with the permission of his Abbot. Successive Abbots have renewed this permission in view of the special circumstances, despite the fact that giving spiritual direction to persons outside the monastic community is done only exceptionally in this monastery.

When Eileen receives our Lord in communion at Mass, she goes forth to meet Him and they enter into a dialogue. During this time, Eileen is not aware of her surroundings. She doesn't know how she gets back to her seat in church. On a few occasions, a young woman in her parish who wanted to talk with her after Mass shook her until she responded.

On the contrary, her spiritual director waited until she spontaneously emerged from her thanksgiving in the Masses he celebrated privately for her. On these occasions, during her communion, he asked her to speak, knowing that in authentic ecstasy, the person is very obedient. He then taped her conversations. These tapes, transcribed and lightly edited, are the substance of this book. The names of persons, and details about them, were omitted, and so were some of Eileen's remarks which, because we do not know the reply of her conversational partner, did not make sense. While these conversations were in progress, her director made notes so that he could interview her and ask her what response had been made to the more significant parts of the conversation. In a few cases which are easily identifiable, Eileen reported to her director a conversation that took place in his absence.

These thanksgivings were recorded from January 1982 to 1987. Those published in this first volume took place before September 1982, at a time when Eileen was a member of the St. John's church prayer group, which met in the basement of the church on Tuesday evenings. Bishop Harrington, then an auxiliary Bishop living at St. John's rectory, mentions that Eileen would give prophecy from her seat to avoid attracting attention to herself.

While it was the intention of her spiritual director to publish this material only after Eileen's death, certain developments encouraged him to begin their publication at this time, without further postponement. Eileen has neither suggested their publication nor objected to it. However she urged her director to give priority to his own publications.

In September 1982 the Meet-The-Father Ministry, whose purpose is to perpetuate her teaching, was incorporated as a religious non-profit organization operating directly under the Bishop of Worcester, then Bishop Bernard Flanagan, J.C.D., who, like Bishop Harrington, his successor, has always supported Eileen's ministry.

Eileen's regular ministry began in October 1982 with her monthly teaching and healing services at St. John's church, where since then they have been held on the fourth Sunday of the month. After October Eileen was called to give services in other churches throughout the country and abroad. Eileen also gave prophecies at the Cathedral on certain occasions and elsewhere; in 1982 to 10,000 people at the National Charismatic Conference in Notre Dame; at the Eastern Charismatic Conference in Providence, R.I.; in Korea as the guest of the National Korean Charismatic Service Committee in May 1986 and May 1989. During May 1989 she spoke to over 80,000 people.

Eileen has always required the authorization of the diocesan Bishop before giving a service, which corresponds with the desire of her Bishop. She also limits her services to those in which a local priest will be present. This book shows how the Father in preparing Eileen for this ministry revealed many mysteries to her, and initiated her into the manner in which she was to conduct her services.

In 1987 Eileen's spiritual director, at her insistence, ceased taping her thanksgivings. The opportunity to do so ended soon afterwards, as her schedule became more demanding, and prevented them from meeting on a regular basis.

THE WAY THE CONVERSATIONS ARE PRESENTED

Five dots indicate a pause in Eileen's speech, when Eileen is listening to her heavenly conversational partner speaking. Very often Eileen will repeat what has been said to her, a way in which she dwells on these words. Bold type calls attention to this fact. In repeating, she sometimes replaces the second person singular, by which her conversational partner addresses her, by the first person.

At times the Father or Jesus will ask her to repeat after Him word for word what He is saying. These words are also put in bold type.

While this book has a unity in its revelation about Heaven and the three divine Persons, it is divided into five parts according to a particular theme treated within that part.

It was necessary to make a decision about Eileen's manner of addressing Jesus as "Butchie." This seems irreverent, and threatens to be an obstacle for many. Reluctantly therefore the editor has replaced this familiar term of address. To understand it one needs to know that before the age of three the Father took Eileen in hand by giving her as a companion, playmate and teacher a child about two or three years older than herself, who grew up with her. This companion said to her, "Call me 'Butchie,' and I'll call you 'Slug.' " A few years later Eileen realized that Butchie was Jesus. From then on she reverenced Him as the Son of God, but she continued to call Him "Butchie."

God's desire to be with us on familiar terms led the Son of God to the womb of the Virgin, to the Cross, and to the Host where

He became our food and drink. After that, is it surprising that to this dear child of His, He is "Butchie"?

END NOTES

1. St. John of the Cross. *Ascent of Mount Carmel,* Ch. 22, No.3–7
2. 1 Corinthians 12–14
3. 1 Tim. 3:15
4. Ephesians 2:20. The footnote in the New Jerusalem Bible says that the New Testament prophets are here referred to (not the Old Testament prophets.)
5. "Prophetism" by Karl Rahner in *The Encyclopedia of Theology,* edited by Karl Rahner, 1975
6. *The New Jerome Biblical Commentary,* 1990, 11:3,4,25, pp.186–187, 199-200
7. ibid., No.4
8. I asked a friend, a graduate of the Harvard program in community psychiatry, Rabbi Earl Grollman of Beth-El Temple, Belmont, MA, if he could supply the reference for this quotation. He said he could not, but that he agreed with it.
9. Quoted in *The Great Reckoning. How the World Will Change in the Depression of the 1990s,* James Dale Davidson and Lord William Rees-Mogg, Simon and Schuster. New York. 1991, pg.257
10. Walter Kasper, *The God of Jesus Christ,* Crossroads. 1983. This is an excellent theological treatise. While it is not written for specialists, it requires careful study.
11. Published by the Meet-The-Father Ministry, 363 Greenwood Street, Millbury MA O1527
12. "It is clear, therefore, that in the supremely wise arrangement of God, sacred Tradition, sacred Scripture, and the Magisterium of the Church are so connected and associated that one of them cannot stand without the others." *Constitution on Divine Revelation,* No. 10.
13. John 10:16
14. "Now all that can exist without charity can be without sanctifying grace, and consequently without goodness of conduct. Prophecy can be without charity." St. Thomas, *Summa Theologiae,* II.II. 172,4.
15. Matthew 7:22,23 See footnote 14
16. St. Thomas, *Summa Theologiae,* III,1
17. Genesis 18:17
18. Exodus 33:11
19. 2 Samuel 7:8,9

20. John 13:25,26

21. *Summa Theologiae,* II.II. 174,3 "Still higher is that grade of prophecy when, awake or asleep, there appears the very guise of God himself [in specie Dei], as in *Isaiah, I saw the Lord sitting upon a throne.*"

22. Luke 14:11. Quoted by St. Benedict in his Rule, Ch. VII.

23. 1 Corinthians 12:31

24. "Charismatic Prayer," a chapter in *Hammer and Fire. Way to Contemplative Happiness, Fruitful Ministry and Mental Health,* Raphael Simon, O.C.S.O., St. Bede's Publications, Petersham, MA 01366

25. 1 Corinthians 12:4-7

3. Bishop Daniel Reilly of Norwich, Conn. and Eileen at one of her Priest Retreats

4. Bishop Willem Michel Ellis, in whose diocese the Catholic Charismatic Conference was held at Aruba, Dutch West Indies in April 1992. Eileen was the principal speaker.

PART ONE:
THE MISSION

1. REVELATIONS ARE COMING
January 6, 1982

THE FATHER TO EILEEN: "Listen well to your director. I have chosen him as your director. Listen attentively to his words. Cut free from all men so that you may live in and for Me. You will flourish in the freedom of My love and you will reach out to all with prayer and love and you will allow Me to function as God.

"I am calling you into a deeper solitude so that I can speak to you and there will be no contamination. My words will fall on pure ears and the secrets of My kingdom will be revealed to you. For too long has man rejected the revelation of his God. This will be the beginning of a new life in God, and the world will know that God is truly mixing with man.

"Eileen, you will make known to your director all that I reveal to you and he will write down the revelations and prophetic messages — and see them come to pass — and make them known to the whole world, and the whole world will truly know that I have unfolded My secrets before you. I have never meant to keep Myself aloof from you [from mankind].

"Child, you will pay a price, the price of love. Never have I revealed so much since Thomasino [Thomas Aquinas] laid down his pen. In the simplicity of your heart you will take it up and reveal My knowledge to My people. It is very important that you leave nothing out. Repeat everything that I tell you to your director."

THE FATHER TO EILEEN'S DIRECTOR: "My son, I tell you over and over that I love you beyond all understanding. I will show you some of this love in the revelations that I bring to you through this Child. You will hear the Father's theology as you have never heard it before, in a simple manner, in a true manner. I will unfold to you the mysteries of My knowledge because man has put a divider between us. You will listen attentively to My words for I have chosen this vessel with little knowledge of books so you will see the truth flow from her very soul as taught to her by the Father. Be attentive, be open, trust and believe."

THE FATHER: "Eileen, My daisies are being choked by weeds. I will pick out the weeds, I will pull them out by the roots. The daisies that stand straight will adorn the altar. I do not want you to have sorrow in your hearts but the day of reckoning is coming when I will separate the daisies from the weeds, the sheep from the goats.

THE FATHER TO EILEEN'S DIRECTOR: My beloved son, you will stand tall and free as a daisy. Other brothers will come and try to choke out your learning, but you must stand tall and straight."

THE FATHER: "Eileen, I love you so. I have so much to teach you, to reveal to you. I do not wish to tire you, but I am opening to you a new world. I have brought you this far hand in hand, because you have been open to Me and have not blocked Me out, but have accepted Me on My terms in childlike simplicity, hanging on to My very knees for strength, looking into My very eyes for conviction, knowing that I love you and that you truly love Me, not just because I am God, but you truly love Me as your father. No greater joy can one give Me."

THE FATHER TO EILEEN'S DIRECTOR: "My beloved son, I speak to you this moment as an ordained priest of the Almighty, a consecrated son. My people have drifted so far from the Father's heart, from the Church, from the Savior's arms. I am giving My people one last chance to turn to Me. I know as humans you demand signs and I melt to this. Yet I say to you this night, those with hardened hearts will not be touched by this.

"There are trying days ahead for the Church. The Vicar of Christ will shed many tears and be the victim of many blows. His first blow will be struck by one of his brothers in his household. Woe to the son of man, for they are rejecting their God." *[The Father then urges rejoicing because those who truly love Him will be his comfort, joy and repose, and those to whom they reach out by prayer and sacrifice will be saved.]*

2. FREEDOM. THE HUMANNESS OF GOD
January 17, 1982

Jesus, look,that bird is flying from flower to flower, so happy. Why is he so free, so happy?..... Yes, I know my birds depend on me for food, but they're happy..... Why aren't they free?..... Are these birds so free, because they depend on You? Does that give me freedom, to depend wholly on You? Is that why I'm so free in the meadow, I'm not tied down to men, I'm free?

EILEEN TO HER DIRECTOR (later): He said the birds in my yard become captive. They know where the food is. They come to me to get it. My people tie me down and are not free themselves. If they went to Him they would be free. I am only human. He is unlimited, and can give everything.

Jesus, how can I be free, totally lost in You and still function as a human?..... This human separation gives me such pain...... There wouldn't be such a division if I were free as this bird, depending wholly on You. Then I, too, would be totally free.

[Note that Eileen frequently repeats the words of Jesus or the Father, and not only when one of them asks her to do so. In doing so she sometimes exchanges the second person for the first. Thus if Our Lord says "Then you, too, would be totally free," Eileen in repeating this to herself says, "Then I, too, would be totally free."] I'll isolate myself. You ask me over and over, Jesus, but this is so hard. I feel so mean..... **So long as I am charitable and kind, I am not mean.**

Look at that bird. I never asked You the color, I felt it would be an invasion..... What color is it?..... **Katika**, katika, katika. She turns to look at me. You call them by color?..... I'm not very bright, how can I learn all these things when I come to You?..... **The knowledge of the kingdom will be infused by the Father.**

Jesus, how is it that we don't see You laughing?..... **They forget the humanness of our God.**

EILEEN TO HER DIRECTOR (later): He said we don't see Him laughing because artists have painted Him as a serious God. He cried, laughed, worried. He said: **"You must make My people know I was as human as you, I cried, laughed, prayed. The Son came to earth to become a human."**

If we allow Him to share in our laughter, joys, worries, we will get to know Him. Then Jesus will unite us with Himself. The Father wants us to be one with the Son.

Jesus, look! The Father is here..... You knew it all the time! Father, You never intrude. We love You so much. I wish I could be here forever..... Yes, we will come. Jesus, You sit here, and I'll sit there..... Yes, My Father, I could listen to You forever..... Thank You, my Father..... I really didn't want to mention it..... I know You know everything.

EILEEN TO HER DIRECTOR (later): My offering of my sufferings for priests pleased Him. So did my praying for the people who called, instead of speaking with them on the phone.....

I'll try to do better this week.

THE FATHER: "She suffers and the Father weeps when His child suffers. She gives herself for the beloved priests. I have called her unknowingly to herself. I infused her with great love for the divine Son, great love for His Passion, great sorrow. He has chosen her as His bride in love, joy, suffering. Together they suffer for the sins of the world. She seeks it not, nor do I, but My heart goes out to her. The Father needs generous souls to bring the world together. Souls with free will; reparation must be made by the free will of man. Man must desire to repent. Only this will appease God.

"I am not a harsh God, but a just God. Again I say to man, I have chosen this child because of her love. I am hurting again as though it were My Son suffering. The Father is hurting to watch His child suffer. Woe to the sons of man who cast her suffering by the wayside. My children must know how much I love them, and I come through the simplicity of a child. Reject it and you reject Me.

"Eileen, look into My eyes."

My Father, why must I repeat everything?..... All right, I will. All the love I see, so beautiful, He adores me, He loves me. I am special to Him. He's crazy about me. I can tell it in the depths of my soul..... I see a father I adore and love. I see all the love You hold for me. All right, I will repeat.

THE FATHER: "Eileen, you must tell My people how much I love them, how much I want to be with them, a part of their life. Not only as a God, this separates, but as a loving father, a daddy as you call Me, so they can relate to Me and I to them. If they fall in love with their Father Dad, I will not hurt them. Tell My children I want to reveal Myself to them if only they will let Me."

Father, how can we let You? Remember, You kept Your distance from me..... I didn't realize it was my doing. By love He will reveal Himself. If we love one another, as Scripture says,

He will reveal Himself to us. We will not see Him, but we will feel His goodness and the Spirit will work through us.

EILEEN TO HER DIRECTOR (later): The Father said, "All are not going to see Me as you do, Eileen, but they will feel My goodness in the beauty that people are reflecting."

The angels who are always chanting, praising and worshipping God stop to listen when I am with the Father. I said: "Father, they are listening to us!" He said, "That's all right." They love our relation. Benedict and Gregory love it too.

THE FATHER: "Eileen, real love is care of oneself —unless you love and care for yourself you cannot really love your brother — and of one's brother in kindness, gentleness, meekness.

"Eileen, if you are always there when they want you, you will get bogged down. Love them by prayer. It is not important to make contact all the time with man. It is not important that they know that you are always praying for them. They might reject that as humans. When they get to Judgment and are with Me, they'll know all the prayers you have said. Let your thanks be in Heaven. If they reject you, I will never reject you.

"In days to come man will reject brotherly love and meekness. They will think it is weakness. Parent will turn against parent and child against child. You must show love to be My daughter. Only love can bring the world to order."

Such a little word.

"Yes, the whole world will be brought to order by love. When you are hated, respond by love. This will set them back on their heels. It will make them think. It makes an impression. You will be respected, perhaps not outwardly but inwardly, first by God, then by man. All virtues come with love. Hatred closes the door to all virtues. Remember the bird in the meadow, free to fly and free to love the Son, and depending only on Him. So with you."

Father, you tell me too much. I can't digest all this. I love You so much. How long this terrible hurt of a human separation? I like being with You, my Father. I love Your love. Each time You are more beautiful than before. Veils keep falling. I don't see them or touch them, but I know they fall. I see You more beautiful with so much more majesty. I know I can't see You in Your splendor, I would die. But I love You just as You are, just the way You are.

"The closer you come to Me, the more You will please Me and see things as the Father sees them. Little by little you see Me more, the purer your thoughts. Purity draws you closer."

Will I ever see You in Your splendor?

"Eileen, even in Heaven there will still be majesty that is beyond you. You will see My beauty to your fullest. Can one depict the full ocean when the moon rises and the beams of the moon cross it? Birds find the air wherever they go. Come, let Me love you. There is no escape from Me. I pursue you, as the air pursues the birds."

3. EILEEN WILL MAKE THE FATHER KNOWN
January 24, 1982

Eileen and Jesus were together at the Communion. They sat beside a brook, which reflected their countenances. Jesus threw a pebble into the brook. Because of the ripples their faces were distorted.

Jesus said: "This is what Capi *[Capitano, the little captain, Lucifer]* is doing in the Church. He is distorting the image of the Son and His Father by the ideas which liberal theologians are introducing."

The Father told Eileen that He was giving her a new mission, to make Him known to his people. He explained that this was their last chance. He had sent His Son and He had been rejected; His Word *[Scripture]* was distorted so that the Father and the Son could not be clearly seen in it. His Son's Eucharist had been despised and ridiculed. He had sent His Son's Mother and she had been rejected. He had sent His Spirit [the Charismatic movement] with the same result.

Now He had no one else to send. He would come Himself through her. She would make Him known to His people. If they rejected Him, then the river of hope separating the two contending forces would dry up and Armageddon would take place. He showed her the two forces: those in black, ugly, under their leader, Lucifer, and at the head of the forces of God, Michael. Michael would do battle with his sword and the defeated army would go into eternal loss.

Eileen pleaded that she was stupid and unable to make Him known. But at His insistence she said she would do whatever she could. She appealed to Him on behalf of the people, saying that she had not known Him until He revealed Himself to her. The Father replied that He had made Himself known to her because she had hungered for Him. She asked Him to give the same hunger to his people, and reminded Him that her hunger for Him and for the Eucharist had come from Him. He said the people put obstacles in the way. They had the same chance to know Him as she had had.

She pleaded with Him not to let the river of hope dry up, or not too soon. She said: "Don't talk to me as God, You make me tremble, I don't like it. I like you to talk to me as my Father." He said that if His people reject Him as Father, then there is nothing else but His godliness for them to face.

Thomasino encouraged her by promising to help her make the Father known. He said He would come daily. She said that she would write down what he told her.

4. ACCELERATING THE GRACES
February 7, 1982

My Father, I am delighted that You are allowing my spiritual director to share in these beautiful mystical experiences. [Her spiritual director asks her to speak after her communion, when she *loses contact with her surroundings. He then tapes what she says. These tapes, transcribed and lightly edited, are the substance of this book. In a few cases, Eileen has sent her director a tape which she made after speaking with the Father or Jesus. These are identifiable.]* Because sometimes, my Father, I forget some of the things You say. They come back to me later, but I think it is right that my director should hear everything.

[As Eileen's vehicle is climbing a hill]: "**Eileen, see how steep this hill is. The car keeps climbing and climbing, because you put your foot on the gas to give it more speed. This is how it is when you reach out to your friends through prayer and sacrifice in silence. You accelerate. You send the graces to them much faster. Prayers reach out to them much faster, and help goes to them much faster, because you are obeying the Father's will.**"

[Later, as she goes down hill]: "**See how fast you go down the hill? You don't have to step on the gas. This is how people backslide if they depend on humans, any humans. They must depend totally and completely upon God.**"

In my love-time with Jesus *[upon receiving Him in communion]*, I ran to Him with my arms open, and it's as if we are in slow motion, and not stepping on the ground. He's running towards me, and His beautiful hair is flowing, and His robes, whiter than white, are flowing. Then He embraces and kisses me. His lips are on mine, warm, sweet, and wonderful. I fade through Him, completely lost in His love, a love beyond all understanding.

THE FATHER: "**Eileen, you will speak with the tongue of power, wisdom, and knowledge to your people, My people, and give them a teaching. I will speak so powerfully through you, Child, that people from all over will come to listen to you. I will not change your simplicity or your childlikeness, but I will speak great wisdom through you.**"

"**Eileen, do as I say and be free and be open to My divine Holy Spirit. Through the wisdom and the love of the Father, you will touch many souls and bring them back to me.**"

EILEEN TO HER DIRECTOR: I want so much to bring people to know my Father, to make them love Him as I love Him. To rub His cheeks and pinch His nose and hug and kiss Him and bring Him joy and peace and happiness.

5. THE HEARTBREAK OF THE FATHER
February 14, 1982

Father, I am going to try to put on tape what took place last Sunday. I can't remember everything. At one point, my Father said: "**Eileen, I plant so many seeds of love on earth. Jesus was the perfect example of love, of meekness, kindness, understanding. Yet, my children have been digging them up by the roots, and casting them along the wayside. In return they have been planting seeds of hatred, jealousy, envy. This hurts the Father's heart very deeply.**"

Another thing He said was about pain. I was walking in the meadow with Jesus. He was holding my hand tightly, so securely. With Him I always feel so safe, so loved. I feel a spirit of trust and understanding between us. He never lets me down. Well, Jesus was picking flowers for me, and I said, "O Jesus, my foot hurts. I must have stepped on a rock." He said: "**No, Eileen, you didn't step on anything. Back in your human world, your foot hurts so badly that you have brought it into this world.**" *[Eileen had spicules of bone in her heel. The orthopedist wished to operate, but her oncologist would not allow it, for fear that an operative procedure would activate her malignant melanoma of the lymph glands.]*

The Father said to me, "**Eileen, have Jesus tell you more about your heel.**" I said, "Jesus, stop picking flowers for one second, and tell me more about my heel." He said: "**Eileen, when I carried the Cross, I stepped with My right foot on a very sharp rock. It pained Me terribly. The pain went up through the muscles and into the knee. When I was hanging on the Cross, Eileen, with the excruciating pain in My hands and My feet, I was still aware of** the terrible pain in the heel. Your heel is a remembrance from My Passion. They can say it's bursitis, broken bones, splinters, but, Eileen, it's a mark of My Passion. Use it well for your sanctification and for the sanctification of souls."

I was delighted, Father. Then Jesus handed me a bouquet of flowers. I can't tell you the colors of the flowers, they're colors I've never seen, and they have no name, at least in our world. One flower looked like a big enormous rose bud and it was closed. But with a touch of the Savior's hand, it gently unfolded like a beautiful rhapsody or melody. The aroma that came from that flower was breathtaking.

The flowers nodded at Jesus. The blades of grass nodded at the Lord. The trees bent and bowed before Him. The babbling brook seemed to call His name and speak to Him. At one point I said, "Father, the brook sounds like it's speaking." He said, "It is, Child." I said, "But Father, the brook has no soul, how can it speak?" He said, "Here it can, and it's saying, 'We adore You, Lord, we adore You, we praise You, we bless You.' " It babbles on and on.

The fruit is beautiful. I know it's fruit without being told. The shapes and colors are different from ours. The ones I tasted were delicious, sweeter than sweet. Everything is so beautiful in this world, that I truly hate to come back. Yet I know in coming back I have time to make myself better for my Father.

My Father said: "Eileen, you're going to suffer a great deal this coming year, physical and mental suffering, heartbreak for your priests, for My priests. But Eileen, don't think of it as suffering for a minute, an hour, a day, a month, a year. Think 'I will take this suffering, with God's grace, just for a second. It will be gone in a second.' According to My time, it is a second. In human time it seems longer. It will make you feel better, Child, and it will give you strength." I'll say, "Father, with Your help I'll bear this just for a second, just for a second."

The Father said: "You know, Eileen, I have given man free will, and I have never once invaded the free will of man. Yet, man has invaded the will of God. Man has mixed up the will of God." I said, "Father, how can we do this?" He said: "Eileen, it's My will that You live as holy, happy people, loving one another. But do you do this? My people live in fear, jealousy, envy, hatred. So you see that My will was different for them, but they changed the will of God. Isn't this a terrible invasion?"

When My Father was talking about His priests, how they are going to be divided and separated, His eyes began to fill up as He said, "Eileen, I never invade the will of man, but man has so invaded My will." My heart was breaking. Then I began to cry and cry. I love Him so much. I can't bear to see my Father cry. This is why I was crying so bitterly. Sometimes when I cry, I feel as though I will die for love of Him. I am so deeply touched by My Father's tears. He knows this and He held me so very close, while I whispered all my love for Him. I pleaded my case before Him, my case of love, of my being wholly and totally consumed in His love.

When I was going home, the fog made the snow like sparkling diamonds. I said, "O Father, they're so beautiful." He said: "Eileen, your love and unity with the Savior, these are diamonds that you let fall before Me, that you strew before My feet, and I am delighted with them." I was so pleased with the way my Father used the dazzling snow to compare it with the love in my heart, given to Him like sparkling diamonds. This filled me with joy and with peace, and all the way home I kept thinking, "God the Father does not interfere with our will. How dare we interfere with His. His will is peace, joy, love, and unity. And we don't accept it."

It made me sad. That night I went to bed, Reverend Father, loving my Father and hugging Him and holding Him close in my arms. My Father said to me, "Eileen, I want you to see this." In His hands He had a beautiful box. It wasn't made out of any material of earth. It was made of heavy luminous light, like the light of the Spirit that surrounds the Father, like the light and the haziness of my mystical wedding band. I could touch it with my thumb and my index finger. My finger would feel something, yet go through it.

I knew this was a box. It's something mystical and beautiful. Father God said, "**Eileen, Child, open the cover and peek in.**" I opened the cover (gasps) what I saw was breathtaking. They weren't diamonds or rubies or emeralds, but they were glistening and sparkling like something I can't describe. They were so beautiful that I caught my breath and said, "O Father, they're so beautiful, what are they?" He said, "**Child, they're My treasures.**" "Oh," I said, "Father, what a treasure! I have never seen any like them, they are beautiful beyond all explanation. I couldn't even tell You what they are, Father."

He said: "**Eileen, I will tell you. These are your tears, the tears you shed for the Passion. The tears you shed for Me when you see me upset with the world. The heartache, the love that are in those tears! I gather them up, Eileen, and I place them in My box as precious gems.**" I was overwhelmed with my Father.

He took the box and He held it so close to His heart, while He said, "**These are My treasures. You have cried from your own free will out of love for Me, out of love for the Son, your mystical Spouse. Yes, Child, I truly gather them and put them in this box. See how precious they are to Me.**"

Father, this was one of the most beautiful things my Father has done for me and revealed to me. See how He loves me, see how He trusts me, see how He delights in my love for Him. My heart, Reverend Father, is filled to overflowing with love for my Father, with love for my Jesus.

Father, today I was looking out of the window at the little birds. They are such perfect and unique creations of my Father. My Father used them to teach me. He said: "**Eileen, you see these birds, they come and they go. Every place they go, Child, they find air where they can fly, where they can live. There is no escape from the air. They find the air every place, in the pine trees, in the bird-feeder, under the bushes, in the air, on the ground. My** people must be fully aware this is where I am, everywhere. Everywhere they go they will find Me. There is no escape from Me as for the birds there is no escape from the air." I thought this teaching was unique, Father.

I looked out again at a different hour and saw the pine trees loaded with snow and snow in the field, so white, so lovely, so pure. My soul cried out, "O my Father, I want to be beautiful before You as a tall and mighty pine tree, radiating the beauty of the snow upon its limbs. I want my soul to be a field of purity, as this field is a field of purity. I want to sparkle in the light of the sun, Your Son, and have this light, the purity of my soul, shine like diamonds."

My heart was filled with love for my Father. My soul cried out to Him. For a moment I felt a terrible heartache of separation, my human separation from my God.

NOTE: *St. Paul says, "as long as we are at home in the body we are exiled from the Lord" (2 Cor 5:6).*

PART TWO:
THE CHURCH CRUMBLES BUT WILL RISE

6. WORLD WAR III. FAMINE. THE GREAT PEACE
February 20, 1982

NOTE: *The Lord reveals future things to Eileen, it seems, to increase her zeal in carrying out her mission to bring His children to Him. Eileen has gone about this mission without ever mentioning the events contained in these prophecies. The Lord revealed them also to obtain the prayers of the people. To cooperate with this purpose, they are being published now.*

Prayers and sacrifices may alter the prophecies that follow. Jonah prophesied that Nineveh would be destroyed in forty days. Nineveh was not destroyed, because of the repentance of the Ninevites (see Jonah 3:10; Matthew 12:41; Luke 11:32).

I hear that voice echoing through the trees, Jesus. Whenever I'm with You I hear that voice calling me, as if the trees were whispering, and the echo keeps saying, "Speak, I'm listening." *[Eileen's director is urging her to speak. When asked "to speak" she enunciates what she is saying to Jesus or the Father, and her director can then tape it. Eileen does not seem to be aware of this, until she becomes aware of her earthly surroundings. She then realizes that she has been taped. Sometimes she feels this is an intrusion. In 1987 she was insistent about no longer being taped. Accordingly her director ceased asking her to speak during her communions. He felt that this was in accordance with the Father's will. As mentioned previously, soon after this Eileen's busy schedule prevented meetings on a regular basis.]*

I feel so wonderful, Jesus, to come twice today..... Yes, I love to. You know I do, Jesus. These rocks mean so much to me, Love. To be alone with You. To have You so close. Remember how we walked when we were little kids, hand in hand, Jesus?

I was making a tape on "Simplicity" today. Do You like it?..... **You do.....** I think that sometimes we act so grown-up, so pretentious, when we're with You, Love. I want people to unravel with You, Jesus..... I know, but how can we break through this barrier? We have been geared this way, Lord. I tell them that, and I tell them to spend more time with You, Jesus..... I tell them that, what else can I do to make them understand?..... I will, if You wish me to. I know You'll give me the words to say..... **We must get on a familiar basis with You.....**

But, Jesus, in the Eucharist we have to exercise so much faith. I took You for granted. You were my Friend..... **They must realize that You are their friend.** It's rather hard for us in the Eucharist, Lord. If you stuck Your head out of the door of the tabernacle once in a while, it would be easier..... (laughs) No, I don't want to give them a heart attack. Do you think sticking Your head out of the door of the tabernacle would give them a heart attack?..... You better not do it then. They'll all flop over. Then what do You want me to do?..... **I tell them to sit and to be in Your presence.....** Yes, I will, again and again. If You have patience with me, I'll have patience with them.....

Yes, I will, if You'll give me the grace. I know it's there. Whatever You want me to talk about I will.

Jesus, sometimes when the Father speaks to me of what is to come, I do get frightened. I don't want to know what's to come..... But will it make them change?..... **Even if one changes, it would be worth it.** What if we don't?..... I know, Jesus. Every time You tell me this, and the Father tells me, it floors me, Jesus.

Look at the vakies! What are they?..... I thought 'birds of paradise' was just a make-believe name. Jesus, look at that bird now. His colors, his feathers are different. He's looking at You..... (laughs) Can I pat him? O Jesus, he's so beautiful. Can I keep him?..... I know I can't bring him back, but can I put him in my castle? Would he want to stay there?..... He will! O Jesus, that's great, that's great.....

Yes, I did, I talked to him this morning..... He did tell me that. How did You know?..... Well, You know what, I felt his hand upon my shoulder last night, and when I woke up, he was standing there..... Not really. I really don't get frightened. If it were a noise outside I would, but not from Thomas. Yes, he did tell me about it, but You know, my Father told me all about it.....

Jesus, why do we need a war to survive?..... **We don't.** But everyone says we do. They say without the work of the war we won't be able to survive..... I know He has blessed us. Is it because man wants all this luxury? Don't they realize all the luxury they have without buying so much — to be free people?.....

But You or my sons will see it. Thomasino said the Father declared it's definitely coming..... 'Course I worry about them, they're my flesh. I love them, Jesus..... Why would Thomasino wake me up for that? My Father already explained it to me, Jesus..... Well, whom will I tell? Jesus, isn't there some way You could stop it? Must we have this war?.....

Many great men have said there would never be a World War III, it would destroy the earth..... I know it's not from my Father, Jesus. I love Him. I know it is not from Him. Who will start this war?..... Why be so selfish with the oil, what are they going to do with it? They don't give it to us, Jesus, we're not asking for it for nothing.....

The Father said the anti-Christ would rise in Syria, Jesus. You are contradicting the Father. **That one will be Lucifer.** Who will this one be?..... But they're religious people, I know they are not Christians..... I don't want to see him..... (gasps) He's young. He's young. **He will start the war.** Jesus, he has a turban on his head..... **A Moslem.**

Can't You stop it, Jesus?..... Yes, I will make the Father known as much as I possibly can by grace. We will turn the people to love Him..... All right, if He has more to say. Thank You, Jesus, thank

You. Don't run so fast, I can't keep up with You. Hold my hand. Look at Him waiting for us. (laughs)

Hi, my Father..... Many, many things..... Yes, we came to continue it, my Father..... Yes, You told me all about it and Thomasino told me..... I know only as much as You have revealed to me, my Father..... Jesus showed him to me, Father. He allowed me to see his face. His skin is dark, my Father. He has a mustache and black hair. He wears a turban, Father. If you know this is going to happen, couldn't You stop it?.....

I know, I know, You love us, Father. I will repeat my Father. I'm looking in Your eyes, my Father. Yes, I hear.

"There will be a World War III and it will be started by a man who wears the turban of the faith, a Moslem. He will be an anti-Christ put upon earth by Lucifer. Yet there is a more powerful one to rise in Syria, when this one has accomplished his work. He will cause destruction and pain. He will cause heartbreak and tears, and a great persecution of Christians. The earth will tremble with earthquakes. He will be a great ruler of Satan."

"After many years of battle . . . "

How many years, ten?

"Fifteen."

Fifteen years of fighting, my Father? We'll all be dead.

"After fifteen years there will be a great peace, a great peace. The land of terror will fall at the knees of Mary. Her blue mantle will overshadow them, and the red will flow into the sea, and covered by the mantle of blue, they will join the free world in peace and harmony."

My Father, how many of us will be left? Fifteen years! Fifteen years, my Father. It may be a blink of the eye to You, but it's fifteen years to us.

"And then there will be a long, long peace, longer than has ever fallen on the earth."

O Father, I love You. I shiver at the thought of war. Not that I'll be here, but my children will, my Father. I trust them in Your hands.....

Please don't cry. I know war is not from you. I will call Your name and I will try to give the Father to the people. Father, put the right words in my mouth..... I promise You, my Father. Hold me close, please, Father. I do hurt.....

Yes, I know You're hurting too. I'm not worrying about the dead. I'm worrying about the living. The pain, the famine. Famine, Father..... **A great famine.** Aren't those days gone, my Father? Can we have famine with so much food?.....

(whispers) We'll get it too!..... I will, my Father.....

No, I'm uptight..... Thank You, Father. I can feel it touching every fiber of my being. Thank You, my Father..... I promise, I promise.

7. "THE MESSENGER OF GOD"
February 21, 1982

You know, my Father, my consummation lies in You..... No, it's all right, my Father, I feel no bitterness. You know the secrets of my heart..... I know it's my dopey humanness that hurts. I love You, my Father. I love You. I know I can't have attachments, even to feelings, if I am to do Your work..... Yes, **to feel sad is to indulge in a feeling**. I remember that, my Father. I'd rather not talk about it any more..... I don't think I am pushing it in the background. I'll be free to do Your work, I promise You...... I did offer it for her soul, my Father. You know that..... Will all this help me to do Your work better?.....

That's the only thing I have to do. You must give me the grace to do it, Father. Alone I can't, but with You I will..... It's the beginning of Lent. It's OK. Just tell me what You want me to do now. I will do it for Your priests.....

I know, I read about his leaving. Will he come back, my Father?..... It's OK, my Father. I'll tell You this at the beginning of Lent. You know how Chrissie takes the sock in her mouth and shakes it, runs up and down the stairs and through the rooms, drops it where she wills, picks it up when she wills, chews it, spits it out. My Father, I will be Your sock. Do with me whatever You will. Throw me around, run with me, pick me up and love me. Do anything that You will. It's OK, Father. But I hope You will find time to love the sock, to hold her..... Whatever You want, my Father. I know it's forever. You taught me that and I remember it well. I will try so hard to give it to our priests. This season, Father, send thy Spirit upon me, with His Wisdom.

O Holy Spirit, I know You're present, I see Your light, I feel Your power, Your warmth, and that's enough for me. At least now it's enough for me. I feel the love You pour in my heart. O Jesus, can't You feel Him?.....

All right, I will, my Father:

"**This holy season is opening, and if you give nothing else to My priests, you must give them the love of the Father. Not by words alone, but by a quiet love; by your actions; your actions in silence and solitude; by reflecting the Father. They must receive this love this holy season, for there will be a great trial of the clergy after the Eastertime.**"

Father, I can't reach all of them, I can't even reach a few of them..... But how many can we have at St. John's *[at the weekly prayer group meeting]*? How many can we hold?..... How many weeks, how many Tuesdays, my Father? And then Easter...... No, I don't mistrust, I trust You, I'm sorry, I'm truly sorry. I know You have a plan, and I am part of this plan, and You will give me the grace. I trust You, Father. I love You, my Father. I need to rely totally and completely on You.....

I am looking into Your eyes, Father..... What do You mean deeper?..... I see. We are going to erase that hurt, my Father. We will erase it, I promise You. I will begin right in this season. There will be a change. O Father, please give them the grace that they need.....

What is this big trial after Eastertide, my Father?..... But why are You allowing this to happen, my Father? Can't You prevent it?..... I know You don't interfere with man's free will, Father..... You mean by prayer? Is that why You're asking me? It's OK. For sure I will, my Father.....

"There will be talks at the church and you will reveal in a very powerful way the kingdom." You don't mean my secrets, do You, Father?..... Thank You. I don't know if they would understand virtue, Father, but how simply can I put it? They're not nuns and priests, my Father..... I trust You'll give me the words to say. Will the priests be affected by it?...... Is that why You're sending them? Will this have to do with the Eastertide trial?.....

Father, how can I talk about that, and what will it do for them?..... I'll do anything You say, any subject You wish, because I know it won't be me speaking, it'll be the Spirit speaking through me, Father..... Of course I get afraid. My stomach hurts. But I trust You..... I don't mind backlashes, as long as I know I'm doing Your will, Father. If it will help the priesthood, I will, my Father, because it is Your will. Sometimes I get all bogged down. You know I don't like to speak. If they ask me, I feel as though they've been inspired, and yet, Father, I wait for Your word, and then I feel OK. I hate to fall on my head..... I know. Good for humility or not, I don't like falling on my head.....

Well, that's why I'm waiting upon You. I will do it if You ask me..... No, I'm sorry, Father, I don't believe they're always moved by the Spirit. I just think they like to hear good things. I'm sorry, my Father, but when You tell me, I feel moved..... All right, How many priests a week? For sure?..... All during Lent. Wowie.....

Nope. It won't be a burden. I love You. And if it's good for them, it's OK by me. It doesn't bother me. You know, Father, that's one thing that does bother me, am I getting hard as nails? Yet, I hurt so badly at times. To get a whiplash blew me that much!

You once said: **The closer I get to You, the more sensitive I will become.....** I need a contradiction.....

No, I truly hurt if I think I've displeased Thee, or displeased someone. I don't mind people contradicting me. If You want me to give these talks, I know Your Spirit will be there, my Father, and I will do it during Lent, I promise You. But remember, Father, please don't be so hard on us. Stay with us.....

What's that? Oh boy, Capi again. All during Lent?..... I didn't mean to have that in my voice, I'm sorry..... I'm sorry. O my Father, I will walk through hot coals to please Thee..... How I feel right at this moment? Well, I feel that if You find me worthy for this test, it's OK..... You know what I'm made of..... I don't think I'm made of much. But if you find me worthy to go through it this Lent, it's OK..... (long, long pause)

"You will rise gloriously as a messenger to My people. They will know that I have sent You. I have raised You up before them. I have gone into the meadow and picked the lowliest of the flowers. And I have set her on a pedestal to shine before all men. They will weep at the sight of her and they will know that I have raised her up to shine before them. An aroma of love shall flow as sweet as honey to their souls, and they will weep, knowing they had rejected her, this messenger of God, this messenger to My people. And when she lies at rest, I will flood the earth with graces, graces that have never before been seen, and never again will be seen by the eyes of men. A cloud will lower itself to the heads of men and though the sun will shine brightly over the earth the heavens will cry, and in the warmest area of the land the snow will fall, and in the coldest area of the earth, roses will bloom, and the world will know that I have set My flower upon a pedestal and she is coming to Me forever."

My Father, I don't understand Your prose and poetry. I love You, I feel great peace when You speak such beautiful words to me..... Of course I will drink, I really need this peace, my Father.

8. THE CHURCH DIVIDED. DISASTERS
February 28, 1982

I will repeat, my Father.

"There will be a great famine all over the world. Nothing will grow. The whole world will be hungry. All will be lacking in food. The atmosphere will be changing and cause great disaster upon the earth.

"A terrible earthquake..."

Is that San Francisco?

"It will be opened up and swallowed..."

But I can't tell them this, Father. What can I tell them?..... I will tell them to pray, my Father. **You give the warnings to man so they can pray and change things around.....**

"It will be written that God has spoken to His people through one of His little ones, one whom He loved and trusted to reveal His word."

Yes, I can do that. With Your help I can do that, my Father..... You do frighten me. I know You don't do it to scare me. You just want me to warn the world..... What about that bad guy with the turban? Will that be his first act against us?..... Aha, now you let it out! It will be New York..... Wow, we couldn't live under that..... Wow, they were intercepted, but that one got through (gasps)..... I know You don't punish us, I know You made a covenant with us, but all this seems like a terrible thing coming to us: the famine, the earthquakes. That will be the end of San Francisco, New York..... There will be nobody left *[in those cities].....*

How can I tell them to repent? They think they're pretty good right now..... I'll do the best I can, my Father. I'm just one. Nobody even knows me..... **Some will believe, and the word will go from them to others.** But still we're not really important..... **Our prayers are important,** sure I remember that well..... Father, when will all this start?..... **Between 1990 and 1999......** Wowie. Father, I'll still have kids here......

"Even now it's festering. Eileen, I am calling My people to be holy people, true followers of the beloved Son. I am calling you to reveal the Father to all men. This is their last chance. They must listen closely to your words. The priests must be touched, Eileen. They must realize the great gift of their calling. All this war and heartbreak upset the Father's heart, yet not as much as do the chosen sons. They are crucifying my Son over and over again by their false doctrine, their free living. Eileen, I have placed you upon the earth at this time to work with them in love, not to judge them, but to help them to stand straight and tall.

"You have a powerful mission, Child, and you must function in this mission to the best of your ability. My graces will be sufficient. Be strong with them, be firm with them, but let them see your love. They must be brought back to the dignity of the royal priesthood. Eileen, this hurts Me more than all the trials and tribulations that are to come. Again I say to you, Child, this will be a terrible year for the Church. Even now the Church is being divided. Come take a look."

Who are they, Father? There are crosses..... I see bishops and priests! And some nuns, Father.....

Our Church? **They're Catholic people!** But they're bishops, Father, and priests and sisters.....

Father, that's the Pope. Father make them stop. They're hurting him, Father! Please my Father! What are they putting in his mouth, my Father? (gasps) Father, that's Thomasino's book. I saw him writing in it, my Father. They're making him eat it! Stop them, my Father..... Thank you, Father.....

What do You mean: **false doctrine?** They're Catholics, Father..... O boy, Father, there are hundreds of priests there..... I will.....

INTERVIEW

The Father said it would begin between 1990 and 1999. We wouldn't be prepared for the famine, a great famine, here and all over the world. We have no idea this will happen. It has something to do with the planets changing the seasons, a perpetual season of frost and of cold. There will be nothing to eat. A great shortage of oil. No heat.

The war is not going to come till later, because we are going to be fighting about oil. Then the anti-Christ is going to arise from the Mohammedan race, a Moslem. He is going to have a turban and a big jewel looking out from his turban. The people will call it "the eye of Satan." He is young.

The famine comes first, sometime between 1990 and 1999. Then he is going to start a great war. My Father said he is already planning it. They are building up arms.

He didn't indicate who is doing this?

This leader has already been born.

Is he connected with the Russians, the Communists?

No, but he will be. He'll be an anti-Christ. He will work some policies with Russia. Russia will not be able to trust him either. Nobody is going to be his friend. His own people won't trust him, but they'll be afraid of him. He is going to be a powerful leader, and very, very rich.

Will he come from the oil states of the Middle East?

I don't know. He wore a long robe. He will be very intelligent and well equipped for nuclear war.

Is this country already equipping itself?

Oh sure they are. But they don't know that he is going to spring forth as a leader. He is supposed to come from a religious race, but he is really diabolical. He is going to be worse than Hitler. This Moslem is going to fire rockets at us. Our radar will pick them up, and our rockets will intercept them. But some are going to get through and hit New York City.

My Father is saying now *[about "the change in the seasons"]* the scientists, the astronomers, are going to detect this. They will put the world on an alert, but no one is going to believe them.

The earthquakes are horrible. I saw big, big buildings falling down. San Francisco is going to be swallowed up. The earthquake will start on the floor of the ocean. My Father said the floods are going to be terrible. There will be no holding them back. They'll take down buildings and streets and everything. The war will be in progress, which will make it twice as bad.

NOTE: *These events are conditional, that is, their occurrence, extent and consequences depend upon the prayers and conversion of people. They come from the malice of men and the devil and from natural causes. But a divine miraculous intervention limiting or preventing these disasters depends on us. God is merciful, but He is also just. During these events He will protect and strengthen those who love Him.*

9. EILEEN STRUGGLES AGAINST HER MISSION. THE NEW PENTECOST
March 3, 1982

Jesus, I'm really concerned, I'm really worried about the mission the Father has called me to. I love You, Jesus. You must help me with this..... Yes, of course I want to do what He wants me to, Jesus.

I just don't know what to do..... No, He hasn't. He just tells me to speak to them, and I don't know where to begin, Jesus. I don't mean to complain. I wish You would come with me to Him, Jesus..... Of course I trust..... Yes, I am afraid, of course I am.....

Yes, He has done fine until now. But this is an awfully big thing, Jesus..... Why would they listen to me?..... **They don't hear His voice like I hear His voice.** But, is that enough?..... Yes, I know He can do anything He wishes..... Well, it's like going down a blind alley, Jesus..... Maybe so, but I just don't know how to trust more.....

The Father said speak to them..... All right. I understand that, for sure..... Well, because they don't want to follow it, I guess..... But I can't shake them up, Jesus. They won't listen to me, Jesus. I'm a nothing..... I know He knows what He's doing. Jesus, I'm truly afraid..... Of course I'm afraid. Jesus, I'm a nothing.....

Yes, I doubt. I'm a doubting Thomas. But I have good reason to doubt. Look what You're dealing with, Jesus..... No. Nope.....

Nope..... Nope..... Nope again..... Well, You've got it coming. You be the lawyer. You put the case before Him, because I don't know what to do with Him..... Jesus, I know we're in for trouble.

Jesus, You know what really bugs me, they want to be priests, but they want to be priests the way they want to be, not the way the Father is calling them..... Can't You wham them out?..... Well, what about when the Spirit whams us out? Aren't You fooling around with our will?..... Jesus, please help me..... All right, we'll go together. You've just got to help me, Jesus, I don't know how to get out of this one..... We'll go. You better stick up for me. Look at Him, pretending He doesn't know why we're coming.....

Hi, my Father..... I'm not up to anything..... Well, yes, my Father, we did discuss it. Father, I brought Jesus with me because I just don't know how to get out of this, my Father..... Of course He'll help me, He's Your kid, but You know I'm Your kid, too..... Father, You know what we were discussing. We can't put anything over on You..... Father, I wasn't complaining. I was asking Jesus how I am going to get out of this..... Yes, I do. I just don't know how to get out of it, my Father.....

That's OK. You can see the yellow streak all the way to my toes, it doesn't bother me..... Yes..... Father, these are educated men..... Well, I call it educated if you know a lot about books and God and theology..... What do You mean it's not education?..... **It's knowledge.** But they have the answers, I don't, Father..... I know You speak through me. I know I'm not capable of doing anything, my Father, but I am scared. They won't accept it from me, my Father..... Well, that's OK, I'll be a doubting Thomas..... What if I came before You and I told You Your business? You'd say, "Listen here, dumbhead.".....

Yeah, that's what You think. They'll say, "Listen here, dumbhead!" And you can't blame them, Father. I'm just me. Just me. Dumb. Stupid..... But will they see this wisdom?..... Is hearing it enough?.....

"My Spirit will overshadow them, they will know that you speak in My name. It will be honest, it will be simple, and it will dig

to the root of their souls. **They will have a turnabout face and be ashamed that they are brought into the light by one such as you.**"....

No, I'm still scared...... No, You haven't convinced me. Father, I love You, but I'm not convinced..... But Father, You can't tell me they don't know it's wrong. They're just twisting it to their own lifestyle! You've called them, Father, they must have a little bit of this sensitivity in them, a little bit of this love for You.....

You're counting on that. All right. Now You tell me how I'm going to get to them..... Father, we have seven, ten *[priests attending St. John's Tuesday prayer group]*. That's not enough..... What shall I do?..... If You open the doors, I promise. You better not open too many doors, or not too big of a door, my Father. I'm afraid..... Well, You'll just have to make up for my lack of trust..... More than anything in the world, Father. I will prove it, I promise.....

I'll make a deal with You, my Father. Whatever door You will open, I will enter..... Well, if You want to see me fall on my face, OK..... No, it won't be so bad, as long as You're there to pick me up..... The most important thing in my life.....

Maybe we better talk about floods, tornadoes, earthquakes, Father..... No, I don't think it's funny, I just think I want to change the subject, that's what I think..... I know..... Of course I love You..... Yes..... Father, I hear it every day. But what can I do? What can I do? I promise You I'll go wherever You want me to..... I don't care about the consequences, but I'll probably get an awful stomachache..... Well, You know what they think of him. Thomasino knows what they think of him. "He's outdated."....

"If Thomas is outdated I am outdated."

How can You be outdated, my Father?..... Well why don't You tell them this? **If they outdate Thomasino, they outdate You.** Basically, they're trying to outdate Jesus Christ, the Eucharist, the sacrament of Reconciliation..... That's what we call it here..... **It's a sacrament of love and forgiveness.** You know what, that sounds neat. I like that better than "reconciliation," because we're reconciled in love and forgiveness. You're pretty neat..... Yes, I know about the tower of Pisa. Another one of Your stories.....

"The Church is leaning like the tower of Pisa, and it will topple over unless an apostle comes out of nowhere and speaks the wisdom of God. I've reached into the depths and found the least of My little ones. And through her I will speak the wisdom of her God. They will know from whence these words come and in her innocence and in her simplicity and in her love she will speak to the priests."

That sounds very good, Father. Show me who she is and I will follow her..... No way, my Father..... I know You do. And I love You..... You know there are no limits. I love You beyond all understanding..... Now don't start that with me, Your sad face. Father, I love You and I will do anything You want..... All right. I'm looking. I'm listening.

"Eileen, I have called you to a mission, a mission beyond all the strength of a human. But I am not asking you to use the strength of a human, but the strength of your God, the faith of a child of God. There has to be a change in My chosen sons, for the Church is hurtling to nothing. In this coming year, doctrine and tradition will be pulled apart and the Church will start to crumble. There must be this invisible source of faith, holding the pieces together. The priests will turn against each other and build up fortresses against each other and against the Vicar. There will be great darkness and this has now come upon the Church. There will be a great division. There will be warnings, but they will not be heeded.

"Eileen, I have placed you before them as a thread that is so delicate in My sight, ever so trusting, loving, a thread coming straight from the Father's heart to His priests. This love for the priesthood has been given to you, Child, for a reason. I must use you, and you will come around and accept everything I am saying to you. Reach out to them, speak to them what I want you to speak, no more, no less. Give to them, through the wisdom of the Father and the light of the Spirit and the love of the Son, My doctrine, My tradition, in the simple but sound way that I ask you to. They will know through the light of the Spirit you are speaking in Me, with Me, through Me, for Me.

"Child, turn not your back upon Me. You will not carry this weight alone. I will be in you, by your side, with you. I will open doors and you must enter and fulfill the duty of love I have called you to. Eileen, look how deeply you touched the ones you are in contact with."

(long pause) All of them, my Father, are they really touched, my Father? Do they love You more?..... They do? Look at them..... But what did I say?..... My Father, You make me feel so ashamed of myself..... I know, but I do feel ashamed. I do feel awful about it. Please forgive me, Father. I truly understand, my Father. Look at their faces..... Him, what did I ever say to him my Father?..... Oh, my Father, I feel so ashamed. I see now. It's not me. It's You in me. I can do anything in You, Father, for You are in me. Of myself I know I can't..... I guess I was depending too much on myself, and there's nothing much to depend on there. But with You I can do anything. O Father, I see it so clearly now. I do accept it, my Father. No more Thomas. I do accept it.....

Yes, I do feel the peace. The battle is over. I don't know how You put up with me..... (laughs) I love You too..... Is that why, because You know You always win?

"And the shadow of the Holy Spirit shall overpower thee. There truly shall be a true new Pentecost in the Roman Catholic Church if you walk according to the Father's will. You will be led by the Holy Spirit, the wisdom of the Father, the love of the Son, and always with the protection of Mary."

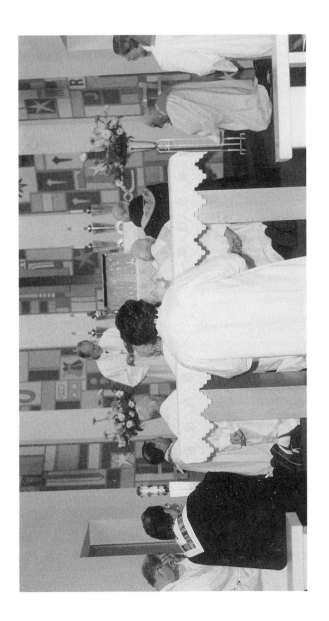

5. Archbishop George Pearce, SM receiving renewed promises of priests at a Priests Retreat given by Eileen in September 1991

6. Monsignor Joseph Pepe, Chancellor of Archdiocese of Philadelphia, with Eileen

PART THREE:
DARKNESS AND LIGHT

10. JESUS PREPARES EILEEN FOR HIS ABSENCE
March 7, 1982

All right, if you want me to sit there and do this, I will. How would You like me to do it, Jesus?..... You like that?..... Let's go down by the water, You can see the good job I'm doing..... You are walking too fast..... No, I like doing it for sure. Can we throw the petals in afterwards?.....

Yes. OK, here's a good spot. Now You sit here. If I hurt You, let me know. Wouldn't a brush be easier? Jesus, how come it never grows any longer?..... You don't have it cut. How come it stays just the same?..... Oh, that's perfection too. It always smells so fresh, so clean. This water is better than a mirror. Look, Jesus, how it falls over Your shoulders. I hate long hair on men, You know, but I love it on You, Jesus. You'd look real icky with a haircut..... No, I don't want You to try it, I just want You to stay this way..... Big deal. I like You this way.....

I know we do look good together.....

Jesus, why do You say that? I would never leave You. I would die first..... But You're not hiding from me, You're right here..... Well, I would wonder where You went. I would say, Look, Eileen, where's Jesus, He's not looking in the stream..... Yes, but if I knew where I would find You..... Right, I'd pursue You. Why are You talking so silly, Jesus?..... No, I would just say You're hiding from me..... Of course I would hurt.....

I know You love me. I would pursue You..... I don't know. Behind every tree, every bush. Maybe I'd just sit here looking into the water and wait to see You turn up!..... I would wait forever, probably. I'd be very sad looking at just me. But maybe someday Your face would show up..... Of course I'd be lonesome..... Nope, I'd never do that.....Jesus, You've given me so much love, it would last forever, just waiting for You. Why are You saying these naughty things? Why are You telling me this?.....

Thank You. But You know that I do..... Yes, I'm aware of it. Jesus, I don't want to talk about that stuff. Remember, I went through that terrible darkness. I don't want to talk about that any more..... Nope, I wouldn't. I know You wouldn't love me less. I would sit here all day, and look into the water, and I would feel lonesome for You. I know some day You'd come back and find me, and I'd be right here waiting for You..... No, I wouldn't. I could never do that. It would be over for me if I did..... I'll always remember this. Forever and ever, Jesus.....

Why do You talk about sad stuff?..... **You'll be with me all the time.** 'Course I know it. Yes, even if I don't see Your face beside me. I look into the waters and see just dopey me...... Why would that make me stop loving You? I would love You more and my heart would beat faster, waiting for the time You came back to me.

Let's throw some flowers in there, Jesus..... (laughs) No, I'm not changing the subject. I want to leave the water while we're together. I don't want to look in and see just me, not even for a little while, Jesus..... We'll throw them in. We'll see who wins. Look how fast they're going. You better get going. They're going to reach that corner before us. (laughs) We win..... Yes, yes, Jesus I do. You know I'll be faithful forever.....

Jesus. You're preparing me for something. Jesus, I don't like what I'm feeling. I'm almost frightened, Jesus. I'll remember You love me..... I will trust You. I don't understand how You could stay away. I could never stay away from You.....

11. JESUS WITHDRAWS
March 14, 1982

I hear the wind rustling in the trees, Jesus. I hear the words over and over. What can I say? I feel Your love, it surrounds me as a gentle breeze. I feel Your kiss, so tender, Lord. My heart pounds so fast within. I am afraid of all the love You shower upon me. Afraid You may take it away from me.

Jesus, Your eyes give me comfort. But they speak to me of a trial ahead. Am I complaining? Do I love You less for feeling so..... I dread a day without Thee. How can I survive without Thee? But I do trust..... It's no secret, You truly spoiled me. Even now my soul cries. The thought of it makes me shake and tremble..... Kiss not away my fears. The love You shower deepens the hurt. It shakes my soul like a thunderstorm.....

I know I need this. You explained it yesterday in the rain. But I don't feel strong enough for it, Jesus..... Oh yes, I'm weaker than You think..... You can if You wish. Strip me of everything, but not You, Jesus..... But why must You do this?..... I don't mean to complain. Isn't there another way You can handle this?..... I know I will be tormented..... I know this, Jesus. Yes, I know all of this..... But why must it be like this? Have I done something..... Thank You, Jesus..... You know the secrets of my heart and of my soul.

Surely You must know, even now I am hurting. Even at the mere thought of it I hurt..... Yes, You know I will. Forever and ever and even more..... No, I won't refuse You. I could never do that..... I will thirst so after You..... I will be so lonely. You're here and my heart aches already..... I know it hurts You too. But why must all good things hurt, Jesus? Look at You! I see tears in Your eyes. But why must we make each other sad in order to grow? I would never leave You, Jesus. Why must You leave me? Why must You hide?.....

I know I haven't. But I can't help but feel that I have done so.....
No. Your love reassures me. Will there be a time when I don't have
to prove myself? I have such a lump in my throat, Jesus. I hurt even
now when You're here. Hold me close..... I must remember it. I'll
remember it. I promise I'll remember it..... I know You do. I'm sorry
for being such a baby. I wish I could trust me like You do. I don't
trust me at all.....

Yes, I will. Like a mighty eagle I will soar the highest moun-
tain peak, the lowest valley in search of Thee. I will feel as a leper
rejected from my Beloved, yet sensing He'll come back to heal me.
I will run daily through the meadows and pursue Thee..... I will be
a credit to You, my Love, I promise. I'll be so good. I'll make You
proud of me, Jesus. I'll make myself so beautiful for You, Jesus, I
promise, that when You find me once again, You'll be so pleased.
In my heartbreak, I'll beautify my soul. In my loneliness, I will
reach out to Thee. In my hungering thirst for Thy love, I will call
Your name. It will fill me, Jesus.

What about our Father, will He too be part of this? Will You
both keep from me?..... All right. You know what is best for me..... O
Jesus, hold me, please..... I love You. You will be proud of me,
Jesus, I promise, I promise..... I am..... I see love, I see love, I see love,
a deep love in Your eyes. An everlasting love. A love that will never
forsake me..... Yes I do trust You. I do trust You..... I see Him by the
tree. No, I won't look back. Don't worry.....

O Father, my Father..... It hurts so much, my Father. I know. I
don't want to talk..... Please hold me, Father. No, I can't look back.
He said not to look back..... I know it will shine, Father. O Father,
please don't You leave me..... Father, please don't leave me. I'm not
that brave to have You both not around..... But I don't know what
I'm made of. You may know, but I don't know..... I get so afraid. O
Father, please help me. Please help me. I hurt so badly. I hurt.....

But it seems forever to me. You've got to remember, Father I'm
a human. It will seem forever. I will die, I'm sure I will die this
time..... I know, I know..... O Father, please help me. I need Your

strength. I need Your strength..... But I just don't understand these crosses, Father. It seems as if my whole heart has been torn from me and I ache all over..... But I have Him. You can't miss something you don't have..... I understand. I trust Father, I'm afraid this time I will die..... But that's for when I die, real die, dead die.....

> **Though I walk through the shadow of death,**
> **I will fear no evil**
> **For He will be with me.**
> **I'm dying to self,**
> **To all the pleasures given to me**
> **By the Father and the Son.**
> **I will stand in faith and love and trust,**
> **For I know that even though I do not feel Him,**
> **Nor see Him, nor hear Him,**
> **In the silence of this death,**
> **He'll be with me.**
> **This will be my strength.**

Yes, my Father, I can remember it..... No, You've always done what is best..... Father, I'm looking forward to it..... No, I don't think it's a game. It's a terrible, terrible thing..... Sometimes I don't know if I want it to be so beautiful. I'd rather have You both with me..... Yes, I trust. Father, I hurt so much.....

I remember so well what I went through. O Father, Capi did an awful job on me. I remember..... Of course I know You do. Of course I know..... I have such a lump in my throat..... I'm such a baby, Father, please forgive me..... I don't quite understand. I'm not virtuous, Father..... I love You. I'll love You forever and ever. I'll never stop loving You, Father.....

Father, I have so much love now..... You promise..... I promise, my Father..... I know You do. I could never forget it..... Oh, please hold me close..... (cries) I'll do whatever You wish. Whatever You know is best for me. I'll love You all through it. I will pursue You forever. If You find it in Your love and mercy, Father, come back to me with Jesus..... Thank You.....

Thank you, Hosches *[Eileen's guardian angel]*. Thank you so much..... Yes, Yes..... Michael, please don't let Him go too far. Watch over me, even if I can't feel or see you, Michael. Don't let me disgrace my Father, my Jesus..... I will..... Yes, I feel it..... Yes, my Father, I do. I love You. I love You forever, my Father. I love You forever.

NOTE: *Besides the withdrawal of their sensible presence and of the continual conversation with Jesus and the Father, Eileen in Lent is plunged into complete darkness and desolation. At these times Satan hounds her, and pervades her soul with such darkness that it seems to her that she has difficulty in believing, hoping and loving. She loses her energy and has to push herself to perform her duties. Despite this, her love grows, insensibly to herself, as also does her desire for her Beloved. And at these times she realizes the depth of her love for Jesus and the Father. This is a little joy, even if unfelt.*

12. THE FEAST OF MERCY
April 18, 1982

Jesus, is this Feast for real? *[the Feast of Mercy].....* Is that why I feel so real?..... Tell me what takes place..... **Like baptism, I can begin anew.....** Yes, I believe it, another grace of Easter..... Then this nun *[Sister Faustina]* was right..... I guess at times as humans we all doubt.....

I don't think I could ever go through it again..... I do feel strong..... I wouldn't do it to You, Jesus..... **Every place I went, You went.....**

Don't tempt me..... Jesus, let's go down by the water..... You're teasing me now. No hesitations, no regrets if You wanted me to come..... I love him, but I'm sure You'll take care of him *[her youngest son, age fourteen].....* Are You trying to tell me something?..... I try to prepare him, Jesus..... I know, it's because I'm functioning..... No, they don't..... Jesus, I love You. Whatever You do in my life is OK with me. You know better than I.....

They look like ducks. What color are they?..... Can I have them?..... Thank You, Jesus..... They know I'm going to own them?..... **Everything responds to love.** Two big surprises in one day..... Is He waiting for sure?..... I know He loves me..... I want to be with Him, too..... Where is He hiding now?.....

Guess who?..... You guessed, my Father. I love You so much, Father. Promise me You'll never leave me again, my Father..... I saw the ducks.....

It's the Feast of Mercy which is like baptism..... Thank You for these gifts..... **Only the beginning.** I just want to be with You, Father, I wouldn't care if we lived in the creek..... I understand it's medicine to make my soul better, more beautiful. But it's bitter medicine..... Yes, I trust You. I don't understand how You could stay away. I could never stay away from You..... My soul is more beautiful? If You say it is, I believe You.....

13. ALWAYS
April 21, 1982

I just like being here and walking with You..... It's just so peaceful, Jesus. Sometimes I don't want to go back..... I know my time hasn't come yet, Jesus, but I feel it is near..... Nope, I'm not afraid.

I wish everybody could see this valley, Jesus. Everything speaks. If I tried to tell them, they wouldn't believe me..... No, I don't try to..... Well, I tell Father *[her spiritual director]*..... Yes, he does. Of course he does. He knows I say what is true..... Yes, he is happy about it..... Well, about everything..... Like this flower. I tell him how pretty it is..... Yes, he does believe me..... Well, the color of it. I know I don't know, but I tell him I don't know..... Yes, I tell him it's sweet, and it's beautiful, and it's different..... Yes, I do tell him about it, but I don't know how to describe it. I just tell him the grass is different.....

Why do You ask me all these things? You know everything.....
Yes I tell him about Saladin *[a black Labrador dog]*, and about the
horses. And about the ducks. And about the fruit, and about the
stream. He knows about our walks, our talks..... As close as I can
remember..... Yes, of course he believes me. He knows it's true..... I
can tell it in his face..... I'm glad You're happy.....

Yes, he knows about the castle..... Well, I don't go into detail. I
tell him about the rooms and the windows, and how the Father
makes it more beautiful with my suffering...... Yes, I told him about
his mother..... You know he was happy..... Well, I tried to. I told him
we eat here. I tell him about the trees and the fruit. I tell him about
the fishes..... Yes, I tell him about those secret places.....

What is it You wish to show me?..... I can't run that fast.....
Jesus, how come I never touch the ground? If I did it back in my
world, they would think it was a real neat trick. I could be in the
circus.....

Look over there..... O Jesus, what are they?..... **Cellabees.** What
are cellabees?..... They're beautiful. They look like our chip-
munks..... How many babies?..... **Nine.** Look at how proud she is of
them. Will she tear at me if I pick them up?..... **There is no mistrust
here.** Jesus, they're beautiful.....

See Jesus, this is what I don't understand, if this is the end and
the beginning, and we can't have babies, how come they have
babies?..... **Because I enjoy them.** Is this what Heaven is all about,
everything I enjoy?..... **She won't have any more. She'll just have
these because I enjoy them.** Jesus, the Father thinks of everything..... No, I just couldn't figure it out because I thought the time
of producing and not producing would be over here..... You mean
it's just because I find such joy in the little ones, this is my joy and
pleasure, and the Father grants it to me. And they'll be babies all
the time, so I can come and look at them..... That's a neat trick. You
think of everything.....

Jesus, they're so beautiful. I hope I remember that, "cellabees." How do you spell that? I'll think of it like a cellar and bees.
Cellabees. We don't have any animals like these. Jesus, they're

so beautiful..... Thank You for showing them to me..... They're mine? **Anytime I desire to come and see them, they're there, and they'll always be babies, and she'll always let me hold them.** Cellabees..... (laughs) Well, I have to repeat, because otherwise I'll forget. You know my mind.

You're so good to me. I don't deserve You, Jesus. I love You so much..... Of course more than life. I do love You more than life. But You are my life..... There's no choice there. This is my world. But I know I'm not ready yet.....

I don't think I'll miss it, Jesus..... Children, yes..... Well, you know I would take this world first, but Jesus, I look into the mirror, I know I'm not ready. There are so many things I have to change. I know the Father will give me the grace. I want to be better when I come to You. I know every day is so precious to me, Jesus. I feel so bad at night. I wish I could have done more. Not to a point of depression, but I want to begin anew each day. I want to be ready for here.

Everything is so beautiful. Sometimes I still do feel like a skunk cabbage in a patch. I know I'm not ready..... Thank you..... I believe You, of course I do. But I also know You're kind and loving and gentle and You know just the right things to say to me. You make me feel so special..... Thank You. Thank You so much..... I do know You mean it. I know for sure. I believe it in spite of myself.....

He really did?..... Jesus, I do love the Father so much. You know, Jesus, last night at the prayer meeting, I was so filled, so overwhelmed with His love. It was at the Mass. At that moment I was praying that I could be with Him forever. It seems as if He were preparing me to receive You. He was ever so present at that Mass.....

I know why He was doing it..... Yes, I know we can't separate You..... I told that to my priests. The presence of the Father at Mass, and of Michael. But last night it was something different, Jesus. I know He is there by faith. But I was so overwhelmed with Him, Jesus, like never before. I felt His majesty in such a different way, such a beautiful, delightful, warm way..... I know there's a reason..... But Jesus, You're going to have to show me how to put it across.....

If You think He's ready. Is He waiting for us?..... **Always.** Always. That's a wonderful feeling, He's always waiting for me. Always. Always. Always. That word is so important right now. He's always there for me. Not once in a while, Jesus, He's always..... Jesus, that is so important to me right now..... All right..... Let me go to Him first, please.....

Father, my Father..... Father, I love You so..... I know You do my Father. Father there is no place in the whole world that I would rather be than here, hugging You.....

I don't feel radiant. I just feel so much love for You, my Father. You are always here, aren't You? Father the word "always" is touching my very soul. It's not sometimes. It's not once in a while. You're always waiting for me, always. What a wonderful word. *Always. Always.* Father why does it mean so much to me tonight? You're always there for me. I've heard that word so many times before, Father. You're always here for me. It seems as though I'm being transformed into it. Father,

I love You so much. I wish I could say more. Do You understand how I feel, my Father?..... Thank you, Father. I'm so glad You can look into my very soul. I wish there was some other way I could say "I love You." It feels so good to be with You, so completely lost in Your love, my Father. Father, it began at Mass last night. This deep, new awareness of You, of Your divine presence, Your majesty at Mass.....

I know, but am I ready to accept it, my Father? I feel at times as though I'm going to burst..... Sure I do trust You. Father, You're so good to me.....

It must come about this year..... Well, I think we go to Mass on Sunday by habit. I think we're afraid of committing sin when we don't go once a week..... I'll be honest, Father. I haven't mentioned that it is the greatest prayer..... Well, if You speak the words to me, I won't hold back, my Father. I will speak to them. But You must put the words in my mouth.

You know what I'm capable of doing..... I trust You. With all my heart I trust You..... No, I won't be afraid..... I know they'll listen, but that's Your work, my Father. They wouldn't listen to a dumbhead if You didn't open them up to me.....

Yes, my Father..... I promise I will..... I love You too, my Father. You look so beautiful tonight, More than ever..... It rings through my heart like a melody, a melody of love. You'll always be there. You'll always be there. In all my joys and sufferings, my tears, laughter and heartbreak, You'll always be there. Always. That word is so important to me, my Father. I can't get over it. It's like a cup of wine, a bowl of cherries, like rubies and diamonds. Always.....

A gift of a word. You mean like the gift of *nothingness?*..... Remember how I rejected it, as if it were an icky gift..... It means so much, Father, when You give me a gift like this, a word. It's unbelievable. Such a priceless word. *Always.....* Why couldn't I feel it before? Why couldn't I rejoice in it?..... I agree. He does do it slowly. Is that what makes it so special..... I will take it into my heart and I'll lock it up there and I'll throw the key away, and only Your touch can get through, my Father. You're always there, always. It's blowing my mind..... That's two wonderful gifts since last night, my Father.....

O Father, I don't know if I can take any more..... I understand..... I'm right there..... Father, I can hear Your heart beating..... (laughing) No, I didn't think You'd be without a heart. But You can do anything..... Nope, I wouldn't be afraid of You if I thought You didn't have a heart..... Father, I love You. I adore You from the depths of my soul. I could rest here forever.....

I'll remember. It's locked in my heart, I will never forget it. Thank You, Father, for the precious gifts..... Yes, I am peaceful, so peaceful, my Father. Thank You.

16. THE EASTER PARTY
April 28, 1982

Yes, I hear, Jesus..... Of course I'm surprised by the beautiful
party, Jesus, but why for me?..... You waited until now?..... I see
all my friends. Such a beautiful surprise, Jesus..... Of course I am,
I'm always pleased with what You do. Look at Thomasino, you
might know he'd be at the table..... Yes, I do love him. He's talking
to Gregory. Do they like each other?..... **Everybody loves one
another.....**

At the head table?..... It's the Father! Look at Him, Jesus. Isn't
He beautiful?..... There's Mary, Joseph, Catherine. Would it be
because it's her feast day, Jesus?..... **Strictly because of Lent.....**
You're so good to me..... (laughs) It's Hosches. There's Michael.....
They're all so happy, Jesus..... I do feel that way, but I didn't know I
looked it. I feel so very special..... (laughs) Thank You..... He's
motioning for us to come.

O Father, this is such a beautiful surprise..... Nope, I didn't
even think about such a surprise. It never entered my mind, my
Father. Whatever You give me is a surprise. Such beautiful surprises..... I don't think I can take any more, my Father..... Am I
dressed properly for it, Father?..... Catherine do I look all right to
you?..... (laughs) You'd say that anyhow..... Thank you. Yes, I truly
believe you.

Father, look at Thomasino. Look at him. My Father, I know he
has a beautiful body, and he's perfect, why do You have him come
to my party looking so fat?..... (laughs) No, otherwise I don't think I
would know him..... Thank You, my Father, thank You so much.....
(laughs) He keeps patting it and telling me, "You should see the
way I look without this." I wouldn't know him, and probably I
wouldn't love him as much. And yet, I would, I suppose. But I love
that big tummy..... No, I don't say it to him.....

There's Benedict, Father. He's going to see Thomasino and
Doctor Mellifluous [St. Bernard]..... O Father, You're so good to me.
I don't deserve anything. Certainly after last night, Father, I was so

aware of my nothingness. I felt so low, almost as if I were cheating my people, Father. And yet, look what You do for me..... Yes, I remember, in my nothingness I find You.

O Catherine, for me? What could it possibly be?..... Can I open it now?..... I'll wait..... Yours first, my Father..... It is beautiful, Father, so beautiful. I can't understand, my Father, Scripture says they have wings, and yet, I know they're angels, and they don't have wings. Remember once You showed me Michael, and he had wings. Look at him. He has no wings right now, my Father..... They're not part of the bird family. Why do you give them wings?..... Oh, Oh. But why?..... Oh, I know they're not humans, and they're not birds. That's for sure. (laughs)..... Oh, I understand now. **To make us realize they can travel fast, in the blink of an eye, and they don't have to obey the law of gravity. They can travel fast and swiftly from one place to another.**

But the Saints don't have wings. Catherine, you don't have any wings under there?..... Nope. I wouldn't know what to do with them, for sure. (laughs) But she has no wings.....

And what about Michael, when he had the wings?..... (laughs) Yes, I'm talking about you..... I understand, Father. I got the message..... (laughs) My Father was telling me what the wings stand for. (laughs) I asked him if you were part of the bird family..... No, you don't look like a bird..... Nope..... I understand, as I understand your size..... Sometimes you make yourself so big, as big as a giant, and then you're a little bigger than an ordinary person. I understand, Michael. Isn't this a beautiful party? Look at Hosches, how happy she is *[Eileen says that an angel has no gender, but she refers to the guardian angel of a woman as "she," and of a man as "he"]*..... O Jesus, you never mentioned it to me this morning..... Of course I'm surprised. I'm delighted.....

Father, You look so beautiful today, more than ever..... (laughs) Of course it's because I love You..... You could never be homely, Father..... Who?..... I see him. (laughs) Martin *[de Porres]*! Why are you hiding down there?..... How could I ever forget you!.....

No, because I love you, Martin. And I love the way you treat the animals. And I thank you for everything you've done for me, Martin.

I'm just so happy. I don't know what to say, Father..... You make me feel like a queen. So special. Last night I felt my loneliness, and today I feel so great with You, Father. And Jesus is with me..... For sure, my Father..... Oh, I don't know if it's a toast or what, but I can feel my heart and soul speaking to You, Father. From the depths of my soul, I love You.....

Yes, my Father, I will open it..... Such a light, my Father. It's engulfing my very soul, my Father..... **Light is wisdom, with it I will see, and I will know the purpose of loving You.....** I feel as though it's engulfing me from my head to my feet. O Father, I know it's priceless and it's special. I can't grasp it all..... How can I thank You?..... It's penetrating my very soul. It's like a glowing white shield. Thank You, Father..... I can't grasp it all, but I will. Oh, thank You, Father. Your present is so unique.....

They look at me with such love, such deep, deep love, such as I have never known..... Thank you, Catherine..... It's up to You, Jesus. Why are You saving it until last?..... All right. I'll open it, Catherine..... I don't know what to say. I don't know what to say..... Oh, I'll treasure it always. Thank You, Father, for your permission. Thank You. O Catherine, thank you for asking the Father..... I can't find words. I've never seen anything like it..... Thank you.....

Jesus, they sing so beautifully. "Now you've grown to an adult size. With nothing but love in both of your eyes. Jesus and Eileen are lovers." They remembered that song..... Forever and ever.

15. GIFTS FOR EILEEN'S MISSION
May 2, 1982

Why did you ask me that? I always listen to you, Jesus..... What do you mean **"very serious year,"** Jesus?..... Yes, I understand that. But I don't like it when you get so serious with me.....

Yes, I know He gave it to me for a reason..... No, I'm not afraid of work. Anything You tell me I will do. I know You're with me..... **He will act through me more powerfully than He does now at the meetings** [*at the St. John's church weekly prayer meetings*]..... Well, of course I do, I don't want them to think I'm always talking, Jesus..... Well, maybe it is pride, but I do feel funny when I have to do it.....

Yes, prophecy, knowledge, they are beautiful gifts..... Well, Jesus, I know these things are good, and they're good for everybody [*for building up the body of Christ*], but don't you think it's centering too much light on me, Jesus?..... Nope. I'm not worried about it. I know what I am. Are you worried about it?..... OK, then nobody's worried about it..... But if He does this, they'll come to me more than ever, Jesus.....

No, I don't like being called a mystic. I know it's not a dirty word, but I just don't like being called that. I get upset..... Well, it's all right if You say so..... I am so aware of my nothingness..... Right, I understand that I'm struggling just as they are, maybe more..... Well, if You're not afraid of it, I won't be afraid of it..... All right, as long as He keeps giving me that grace.

What other gifts could He possibly give me?..... No, I don't look at them that way. I know He's giving them to me to build up the body..... Yes..... Jesus, do You know what that priest does? He singles me out and he makes me feel so cheap and ashamed. [*A priest in the prayer group who calls attention to Eileen's gifts*]. I'm sure he hurts the people around me, Jesus. I do try to stay clear of him..... Oh, I do pray for him. He's always saying something that embarrasses me. I know I need it for my humility. But I don't feel very proud, Jesus. I don't like him to do that.....

Jesus, You know he's not helping me. He can make them resent me..... I know, but I don't know how to tell him that. Why don't You tell him?..... You've got to be kidding! But he's a priest..... No, not really. I'm glad to use them, Jesus. I feel as if I'm pressured to use the gifts. They expect it. This is what bothers me. I know it's my humanness...... And if He gives me that, they'll pressure me more, and more and more. I just want to be me. I don't want to be anyone else.....

Of course I will do what my Father says..... Of course I see You there..... All right. Anything You want, I will do it. I just don't like feeling like a piece of junk being torn apart. Look how that lady pulled my hair. And what about the program, just because I touched it. I feel so awful, Jesus. I know what I am. You love me. You know what I am.....

If You think I can handle it, you know better than I do. Whatever You say. Whatever Father says..... I know You do..... Are You sure?..... Thank You. I wish I could trust me as much as You trust me. I don't trust me at all..... Thank You, that's beautiful.....

Why must their eyes be on me? I feel as if they're invading me, Jesus..... He makes me uncomfortable, for sure..... How can I be myself when I know they're looking at me? Could You be Yourself if they were looking at You all the time? Wouldn't You feel uncomfortable? Picture here, picture there.....

"From this day forward, Eileen, nobody must know of the deep inner spiritual things that you are experiencing, only your director. They will be deep. They will be mystical. A closeness to the Father, beyond all understanding. And while you're here upon the earth, nobody must come to know these things. You will share them with your director, and no one else."

I promise with all my heart. I'll tell him everything..... Is that Him? (laughs) He knows we're here. Father, we were just talking about You, my Father. Yes. He was telling me about it. He said I am to reveal them just to my director. And that more and more people were going to try to discover my secrets.

Yes, I understand..... Yes, my Father..... Of course You can, You can do anything You want with me, Father. Turn me inside out if You wish. Anything, my Father..... Why do You want me to repeat?

"Eileen, never before have I revealed so much to a human being, or through a human being. But I have chosen you because of your love. In this coming year, I will unfold my full knowledge,

wisdom, my kingdom to thee, Child. You must reveal everything to your spiritual director, but to no other man from this day forward. I will reveal many things to My people through prophecy, and you will speak words of wisdom. When your speaking is over, you must draw back into silence and solitude." *[Note: At this point of time, the Father indicates that Eileen is to reserve certain things which will be made known only after her death. He also indicates that "He will reveal many things to My people through prophecy, and you will speak words of wisdom," etc. Hence some things are to be revealed through her public teaching. As time went on, these instructions became more precise as subsequent volumes will show. And it became clear to her director that the Father wants him to publish her conversations with Him without further delay, ten years after they took place.]*

"Child, many will seek you out, but you must not reach out. Isolate yourself. Stay with your God. You will find peace. A tremendous task I place upon thee. My graces will carry you through. This is the hour that God will speak to His people. You will be the vessel. But don't let them contaminate you, Child. Pray for them but keep your distance, or the evil one will use these people to disturb your peace."

Father, why are you telling me all this?..... I don't know how You could use me more, You use me now..... Of course I love You and I trust You. Father You can do anything you want with me..... I know. But I know they won't do it intentionally..... No, I won't. I won't expose myself to it.....I won't let them upset my peace, Father. I will keep a clear head and mind. I'll hear Your voice..... No, not even a kernel of Your word will pass by. I know it's very important to You, or You wouldn't be speaking to me like this.....

Of course I love You with all my heart and soul..... I know You do..... I don't mind the burden, my Father. I need Your grace. I need it so desperately to help me through it..... Mind rejection? No. Just if you do, then I would, for sure..... I know You'll stand by me, Father..... My Father, thank You so much for him. I will tell him everything..... I promise I will.

No, no, it's not a burden. You know me with my reaching out.
But I don't try to play God, Father, because I know You, and I know
nobody can take Your place. But I do reach out to them, to all of
them...... Yeah, they do disturb me for sure. I get so frustrated.....
You're right. You're always right.

You know what? I feel like a soldier on a mission, and I won't
let anyone block it..... I promise You, my Father. I won't tell anyone
a thing. Nothing. I have so many secrets now, I can't dream of Your
telling me any more.....

But that's the gift that hurts me the most *[the gift of knowl-
edge]*. Sometimes I feel as if I'm judging them. They tell me one
thing, and I know they mean something else. Isn't that judging?.....
I don't understand the difference sometimes between the gift of
knowledge and judging. I can see through them, Father..... Well, if
You want it, it's OK by me.....

Father, I don't want them to think that I'm a nut. Sometimes
they look at me funny..... It's not that easy to look beyond it. You
know, You're God. I'm just me..... But can't they realize it's You?.....
Well, I know it's You. I'm a human, I know what I can do and what I
can't do. Can't they look at me and see?..... Well, whatever You
want, my Father. I promise no one will latch on to me.

(laughs) I'm a little bit excited. You tell me so much. It just
blows my mind. How much more can You tell me?..... All right.
Whatever You want.....

Yep. There are quite a few priests now. One week there were
nine. Another week there were twelve..... No, Father, he didn't fool
me. I knew he was a priest..... For sure? My pastor?..... Oh, my
Father, he's never asked me for anything, besides confession,
catechism, bishop's things. *[Eileen was going to confession to her
pastor, taught catechism in the parish, and contributed to, and solic-
ited money for, the Bishop's Fund.]*

I promise with all my heart..... Anything. Anything at all. I
would do anything. I love You, Father. I'm so glad You want to use
me for something, so I can show You how much I love You. I want
everyone to love You, Father. I'll never refuse.....

It sounds real important..... Yes, I know the Church is in trouble. I know, my Father, and it's OK if You want me to help..... Right..... It's all right, my Father..... Well You said the closer I come to You, the more sensitive I will be and the more I'll hurt. So when I hurt, I'll realize that I'm getting close..... I don't see how I could get much closer..... Yes, I remember the veils..... Well then I won't mind hurting, if a veil will drop. It's OK.....

All right. I'll carry any message whatsoever. It doesn't sound so bad when You say You will chastise with love..... I know, Father, please don't feel sad about it. We'll pull together. You the big rope, I the thread. We'll pull together.....

I'm sorry. I didn't realize. I just wanted You to take it away. I promise I'll never ask You again to take it away, my Father. I know it's special, it's unique, and it's for a purpose. I'm sorry, Father. I was only thinking of myself hurting. Please forgive me, my Father. It's OK. Anything You say..... I'll do it, Father. We'll be a team, and we'll do it. Don't feel sad any more..... Thank You, Father. That means more to me than anything in the whole world, Father. I love You so much.....

No, I can't say I'll find joy in it. Not in the thing itself. But knowing I'm doing it for You, I'll find joy..... Nope, I don't know how I ever got along without You..... But You didn't tell me You were there.....

Yes, he does love You more..... I guess he always loved you, but he's on a different basis with you, now, isn't he, Father? I promise I will tell him everything..... **He must know everything.**

No, I won't tell Father X anything at all. I will watch him. Sometimes he makes me feel like a monkey on display. I know he doesn't mean it, Father, but he does make me feel awful, almost like a freak.....

I did enjoy it. I wish the day would come soon when I could sit here and let You speak to me all day long. And I could rub Your cheeks and brush Your hair, never to be separated from You by my humanness again. This human separation is my biggest agony, my Father. Yet, I know I have to grow, and please You more, and make more people know You. And I do need time to straighten me out. You know that better than I do, my Father. And You want this work to be done. We'll do it together, OK?

Well, how far is "**all over?**"..... Why would they want to see me? They may be in for a shock, my Father..... I feel very peaceful, Father..... Nope, I don't feel it *[the weight of the task]* at all. I feel a joy. I never know what You're up to, but I know You're up to something big right now. I can wait..... Not really. I'll be pressing You and trying to sneak around and find out what You're up to..... I mean I can wait, but it won't hurt to push a little..... Nope, I won't take it back. Anything, anything, anything..... Thank You, Father..... You know when You look at me like that, I could never refuse You, never.....

I know. I love You too with all my heart and soul. From the depths of my being I adore You, my Father.

Interview

Eileen, what did your Father say to you?

Well, He mentioned about wisdom, that it's going to take an important role in this mission that He has for me. He says I'll have the wisdom to choose what I should give out and what I shouldn't give out. I have a feeling it has a lot to do with doctrine. Doctrine, tradition, priests, and religious, because the Church is centered on Jesus and doctrine, the religious and the priests.

He didn't give you any indications how people are going to know about you?

No, He just said they will come to me from far off places.

They'll come to St. John's?

I don't know. He said I would use the gifts, the new gifts that He gave me. He told me that prophecy to the people was going to be stronger. And that I must not be afraid to get up to give it. And He said that I have one thing about me, if I speak once or twice, I don't want to speak any more. I feel as if everything's centered on Eileen. But He said: "**If I give you ten messages, you have to repeat** them, and don't care what people say. You speak what I want you to speak, and then withdraw into yourself. Don't hang around to let them all get advice."

He said: "Don't let them come to the house. Don't let them tie you up on the phone, and above all, don't let them drain you after the prayer meeting. Speak what the Father wants you to speak, and then go back to your home. Reach out to them with love. Be kind and be gracious to them, but make them aware that you're not going to stop to talk with them."

In other words, your job is simply to deliver the messages that the Father gives you and then to clear out and not to give advice or counsel to individuals.

Right. He said in their humanness, they'll try to hang on to me. And I said, Well, Father, I know all these gifts are from you. I'm fully aware of this. Can't they see it? He said, "Eileen, they only see as far as the human aspect of things. So they're going to start clinging to you." And then he mentioned that lady who pulled my hair out.

What did He say about that?

He said: "You see how shocked you were about this? They'll do worse than that to you because they're human beings and they're looking for human things. I don't want to put you through this. I want you to give the message, use the gifts, and then retreat as fast as you can to your home. And nobody's to come to the house." They're all finding excuses to come to my house. They bake me a cake. They give me things for the children that they knitted or they crocheted.

They stop and talk awhile?

Yeah, my Father doesn't want this. He said, "Capi can get in there under the pretext of a good angel to disturb you." I can't get back on my schedule. You know, when I saw that lady I lost an hour and a half. He said: "See how nervous and frustrated you were? You know what I expect from you in your household duties. I want you to be kind and do acts of charity, but I don't want you to be off your schedule and frustrated."

Good. Well, are you going to accept this teaching?
I have to.
It's going to cost you one way or the other.

Each person thinks they're the only one and they're draining me, sometimes speaking to me for an hour. But they really don't need it. They don't realize I get hundreds of calls. By the end of the day, I'm worn out. My Father said the most important thing right now is to do His work and to reveal to my director everything that's going on in my soul. I only have the powers my Father gives me. I don't have the powers that they want me to have. My Father has given me gifts for His glory, not to be a big shot. My Father said the gifts and prophecy that He's going to give me for the people are going to be powerful. More and more people are going to hear about the gifts, and they're going to come to St. John's. *[At this time, Eileen is not aware of the monthly teaching and healing services she will give at St. John's beginning in October 1982. In view of the extent and demands of her new mission, her poor health, and the efforts the devil is going to make to disturb her and hinder her work, the Father is asking her to change her practice. He wants her to pray and make sacrifices for individuals, but no longer to see them on a one-to-one basis.]*

He said: "**Eileen, you have to face it, they're coming because of the word of knowledge, and the healings of Jesus in the Eucharist. Don't care how My word is being accepted. Just say it the way I give it to you. Whether they accept it, or don't, whether it's too strong or too weak, you just say it the way I said it, and then block it out. Don't start worrying about it. Just give My message. That's your responsibility.**" It's going to be up to their acceptance to grace if they get it or not. When a speaker comes, he or she may be talking beautifully, but I can see behind it. And then it bothers me. Oh my God, I'm judging. And the Father's saying: "**Eileen, this is the wisdom I'm giving you, so nobody can fool you. You've got to know what's right and what's wrong so that you can do My work. It's not judging. I'm giving this to you. You're looking behind their words and you're getting the truth.**"

Nobody can fool me, and I don't love them less. Somebody can come up to me and say, "Eileen, I had a vision last night." And I can look behind it and see she didn't. I won't say that to her. I'm listening, but I know that what she's saying is not true. My Father said, **"Eileen, if you're gullible and you believe everything, they'll know you don't walk in the Father's light, they're fooling you."**

In other words, you'll discredit His mission if you allow people to....

I discredit the gifts He has given me. They'll say, Wow, she's easily fooled. He said, **"I'll give you the wisdom to answer so you won't have to say, 'I don't believe you.'"** Naturally, He wouldn't want me to say that. The Father deals with people with kindness.

A lady came up to me and started speaking some kind of gibberish, like pig-latin. She said to me, "I know you have a powerful gift of interpretation. Nobody can interpret my tongue, but I know you can." My Father said, **"Watch it. She's trying to pull the wool over your eyes. You know this isn't a tongue."**

So I said to her, "I've never heard such a tongue and I can't interpret it. I'm sorry, you'll have to find somebody holier than myself."

16. THE FATHER'S PLAN
May 5, 1982

It seems extra beautiful here today, Jesus. The atmosphere seems so much brighter, and the aroma is stronger. The flowers are more beautiful..... Yes, I find it peaceful..... But how long?..... No, I'm not over anxious, I know there's so much more I have to do..... You know what it is, it's my human separation.....

I could almost dislike my humanness. Yet, I know in my humanness I can become more pleasing to You and to the Father..... Of course, I love You more than anything, Jesus..... We love Him together, right?..... Right......

I heard it. Some of my friends say that to me, "You see Me, You see the Father." I know You are in Him, but I wish You would make it clearer, Jesus. I know my Father. You're His reflection. But my friends say You shouldn't be singled out from the Father. Yet, I know You as You and I know my Father as the Father, and I know the Spirit. So why do You say "You see me, You see the Father?".....

Yes, I can understand that..... Of course I know there's the Father, silly..... Yes, You prayed, "Father if it be possible, take this cup from me." So, if He was just in You and He wasn't some place else *[that is, if there were not a real difference between You and the Father]*, You wouldn't pray that way, right?.....

Yes, You said, "Father, Father, why have You forsaken Me?" I remember that..... The "Our Father", too. Well, I know all this. But they keep throwing that Scripture at me, Jesus, "You see Me, You see the Father." As if there's no Father. You should have spoken a little more clearly to us.....

Yes, but do they go back to the agony, to the cross, and to the "Our Father"? I'm not too bright, I don't go back..... Of course I understand..... (laughs) No, I couldn't deny Him, for sure. I'm crazy about Him..... I understand that well. "Nobody gets to the Father except You and those You wish to reveal Him to." I know that really well. It's about the only part of Scripture that I do know well.....

Jesus, why did it take You so long to reveal the Father to me? I didn't see Him in You..... Well, I didn't know I saw Him in You. I just saw You..... After our marriage?..... That's beautiful, Jesus. That's really beautiful..... I really do. I do appreciate Him more. He was worth waiting for, for sure..... No, not that I don't appreciate You. You know that I do..... I love Him so much, Jesus. I love the way He looks at You, and the way You look at Him..... Thank You. I can't wait to be here forever either. I know there are so many things I have to straighten out.....

Yes, I will. I try to, Jesus. But every time this Scripture comes up, they throw it at me..... Well, send the Spirit to me and put the right words in my mouth..... Right. I've even had priests say this..... Well, why can't You reveal the Father to them?..... **They don't even know the Son.....** How can a priest not know You, Jesus? They bring You to the people..... **The Father gave them this power..... The Last**

Supper..... But then they believe it by faith..... No one will get to the Father then..... Well, some of them, but I can't really say they do pray to know the Father, Jesus. Yet, I heard more about Him in the last year from them than I've heard before, so You must be revealing Him to some people.....

Oh sure, I can tell whether they know the Father. They talk about Him with such coolness, almost as if He were a judge, which He is, but without tenderness, love..... Look how You talk about Him. You radiate such love, Your face is beaming, Your eyes are dancing when You call Him "Father"..... Oh, I hope so.....

Hold my hand. You have the knack of running ahead of me..... What are they? They look like our jack-in-the-pulpits..... They're beautiful, Jesus. They look as though they almost understand me and feel me. Everything seems so beautiful here, and so loving.

Yes, I see Your face *[reflected in the water]*..... Look at that. It makes You look as if You had creases..... For sure I will..... Don't we look good together?..... Thank You. (laughs)..... If I kiss You, I can't see You. I want to look at You in the water. I want to see how we look together.....

Are they like our lily pads?..... Will they be here forever?..... That seems like an awfully long time. Jesus, when I'm here, will I be bored? I like being here, but there's so much to do in the world..... Well, You know: things..... **What things?** You follow me around all day. You know what things. Washing and cleaning and cooking and dogs and cats and birds and rabbits and everything. Stores and markets and fairs. None of that is here, what will I do? Part of the time will I be bored?.....

(laughs) No, I don't think You're a bore..... I know You can..... It's just so beautiful. But many times things are beautiful and you get tired of them..... **Even that is from original sin: not to enjoy beauty to its fullness. To tire of something can be the consequence of original sin. There's no sin here, so I won't tire of anything, ever.** I'll just go on, and on, and on.

No, I'd never tire of You..... (laughs) I'd never tire of Your loving..... Nope. How could you tire of the Father?..... No, Jesus, I could sit at His knees all day long..... No, He wouldn't even have to speak. Just to be in His presence..... Of course I love to be in Yours..... I'm glad You do. I don't see how You can put up with me.....

I guess I didn't understand your love then..... The best romance in the whole world..... I don't have to tell You, You can read the secrets of my heart..... (laughs) I think he would ask Juliet that question..... I love You, Jesus..... You are my mystical Spouse forever. I thank You for loving me so..... All right, if You want me to. (repeats)

> "Before the age of three,
> I held your hand and led you closer to Me.
> I wiped your tears and I kissed your bruises away.
> I was preserving you for our wedding day.
> I guarded you as a precious jewel.
> You are My treasure,
> Given to Me as a gift from my Father.
> I protected you as a mighty warrior.
> I wooed you into the nest of love.
> I know the Father watched from above
> As I pronounced the words,
> I love you.
> "I saddened when you pushed Me away.
> I sat in dismay when you turned from Me
> To run away.
> You wanted no part of this love..."

O Jesus, you make feel funny inside. I just can't imagine deliberately running from You..... But You pursued me..... I truly love You, Jesus, with all my heart and soul.....

Jesus, that's the Father! Come, we'll go see Him.

(laughs) I bet You thought we weren't coming, my Father..... You were really enjoying our reminiscing, Father?..... Yes. Where are You going, Jesus?..... (laughs) OK.....

I want everyone to know You, Father..... Well, You know what brought it up, it was because of Scripture. Jesus said, "You see Me, You see the Father.".... Yes, I understand it, for sure. But I guess some of my friends don't understand it..... They say, "If you talk to Jesus, You talk to the Father.".... Yes, I understand it..... Every time it occurs, they bring it up..... I know. Jesus told me that. I feel so bad for those that will not know You. It's unbelievable.....

Oh, I do feel very special..... I try to tell them about the Father. Some of them are really loving You more than ever. And I think those that don't, my Father, it's because they don't know about You. It's like when I didn't know You and I kept complaining about not knowing You.....

You better send their angel with more grace to them..... Well, there are just so many things I don't understand, Father. I don't understand people really believing Jesus is in the Eucharist, that it's really Jesus, and then not going to receive Him.....

For sure I have a battle going to Mass in the morning, but by Your help, I win the battle. I can't understand loving Him and not going to Him..... I know it's because we have to learn. Father, You've helped me so much, couldn't You help them, please. I want them to know Jesus more and to receive Him more. I want them to know You, Father, to see how beautiful You are.....

"Eileen, I have placed such revelations in you concerning the Father so you can reveal your Father, your Dad, to My people. Eileen, never have I revealed Myself to any man the way I have revealed Myself to you. I have watched over you from such a tender age. Now you have come to Me, and I have revealed Myself to you. This is the hour the Father will be made known to His people.

"Most of all, Eileen, my priests must know Me. I have chosen you, Child, for a reason. You have not studied the great books. Your knowledge is from Me. They will see Me in your face. They will hear Me in your words. Eileen, this is the hour of the Father.

"You will be like a boat sailing through life. The world will be the sea, and the ripples you will leave behind will be 'love the Father, know the Father, become engulfed in the Father.'

"The Son has come to reveal the Father to His people, but they are not seeing Him, they are not hearing His words.

"Eileen, nothing happens in your life by chance. I have a perfect plan for you. Be open to Me. Don't leave My love. Here I will speak to you. The wisdom of the Holy Spirit will overshadow your director. He will understand you. I will give him the wisdom and the grace to understand what I have planned for your life. Eileen, begin isolating yourself from all men.

"A powerful message will be brought to my people when you go to Indiana." *[To deliver a prophecy to 10,000 people at the National Charismatic Conference.]* "Be not afraid to speak. Remember the Father's glory is at hand. Never be afraid to speak the truth of the Father...... "

I feel such love for You, Father. You draw me to You. O Father, I adore You..... I will, I'll make You known to my people. All I want is for everyone to love You, my Father. That's all I want, that people love the Father.

INTERVIEW

He said I must isolate myself in silence and solitude. I know what He means. If I am in silence and solitude I'm recollected in my Father. I'm not frustrated by the people, and here He can work with me. He has a plan for me. You know this. He wants me to reveal Him to His people. He wants me to reveal the power of Jesus in the Eucharist. He wants me to do this for Him. I'm a messenger, that's all. Only a messenger.

17. MOTHER'S DAY. THE ANGELS. THE ROSE OF PURITY
May 9, 1982

You make me feel beautiful, important..... As long as I'm important to You, nothing else matters..... What kind of surprise? I don't know if I can take another..... Behind the tree? All right. What could possibly fit behind that tree?.....

What's going on, Jesus?..... But will I fall if I sit there? It has no legs..... (laughs) I trust You, I don't trust me..... Daddy made it! For me?..... Aw, look at them all. What are the instruments they're holding?..... I feel like queen for a day.

I've never seen anything like them. Jesus, they sing so beautifully. The words are not our words, but I understand everything they're saying..... Jesus, they're beautiful..... It's unbelievable..... I've never heard such music. Thank You. I wish I could tape it and bring it home..... Enchanting isn't the word for it..... Yes, better than opera..... Thank You so much.....

O Jesus, how can I thank You?..... I've never seen such beautiful instruments. Never..... Thank you..... Of course I'm pleased. Who suggested it?..... **You did.....** (laughs) You're wonderful, too..... I feel so unworthy, and yet, so special, because You're beside me..... And You're happy doing it for me..... O Jesus, my people don't know what they're missing. If only they knew, then they would cling to You..... (laughs) I know that for sure, they wouldn't believe it. Maybe they wouldn't understand.

O Father, it's so beautiful. I truly don't deserve it, my Father..... I know, He told me it was His idea, but He asked Your permission. You didn't have to let Him do it. I thank You both.....

What makes this Mother's Day so special?..... Thank You, Father..... (laughs) He's like the conductor. I thought he was a warrior, Father..... I know, but what amazes me most, my Father, I understand the language they're singing in..... It's so beautiful. I can almost see the words coming out of their instruments.....

Of course I'm in awe, I've never seen anything like it..... Yes, it is a day of surprises..... Yes, it is a day of love..... (laughs) That's all right. I'll be open to those teachings, for sure..... Yes, I did relax today, my Father..... And this is the peak of it. It's so beautiful..... Thank You, Jesus. Just to be between the two of You, I feel so wonderful..... Thank You, Father. That's the first time You've ever said that..... **Because He's Your Son.....** Thank You, Jesus..... Yes, I do..... I love You both..... You're my Spouse. And You're my Daddy.

It's a wonderful show..... I can tune in at home, but I'll never get this..... Look at them..... Isn't that wonderful..... (laughs) **They are doing it just for me.** Thank You..... Hundreds of them, my Father. Do they have to practice?..... Wow. There are so many things I don't understand, my Father..... I'm just accepting everything You place before me. Delighting in it..... Yes, I see some I know: Michael, Raphael, Gabriel, Hosches, Meleika. I guess that's all I know. Thank You, Jesus. It's too much for me. I'm enjoying it for today.....

Listen to that: "Rejoice in the God who has created you, and the Son who has espoused you, and the Holy Spirit who is lighting up your world." Just for me..... Aren't they wonderful?..... O Father, do they know how I feel? I can't thank them enough, will You thank them, my Father? You too, Jesus?..... Aw. Thank You..... I can't wait until I'm here, either..... (laughs) Father, I promise You. And I thank You for this day.....

"If we had hearts, they would speak of our love for you. Let our music be the beat that keeps thee alive forever. With holy expectation we await thee." It's beautiful, Father..... Thank You, Jesus.....

My Father, I come to You now..... Yes, I love You..... No one has as much as I have..... You're all that matters to me, my Father..... Who has as much as I do? You spoil me, Father..... Thank You. Thank You.....

Yes, I would like to see her. Because this is a special day, my Father..... Another happy feast day..... Thank You for coming, Mary..... It wasn't as much as you deserve. But I want you to know how much I love you. You are truly my Mother and I need you so much.....

What is it?..... It's beautiful..... What color is it?..... Thank you, Mother. Thank you so much. This will be in my heart always. It will bring me great peace. Thank you, Mother.

My Father, I thank You. It's more than I've ever dreamt or expected..... Yes, I am in peace..... I love You, my Father, and I'll never forget it..... Thank You.

INTERVIEW

It was a different kind of thanksgiving. First Jesus was telling me how much He loved me. He is truly pleased with me. Sometimes I feel as if I've not pleased Him, but even then He's pleased with me. And then He said He had a surprise for me behind the tree. And I said, "Jesus, what surprise would ever fit there?" The tree was only so big.

When I went there, there were hundreds and hundreds of angels, and they all had the most beautiful instruments that I've ever seen. Not like ours. More like — sometimes you see an angel with a harp? Although, they're not harps, it was different. And they were going to put on almost like a musicale for me on Mother's Day. And they were all so excited, Jesus said. They were preparing for it. And they sang.

Did they practise to prepare?

No, they didn't have to practise, the Father said. Jesus said they were so excited they were going to do it for me. And they sang in different languages. It all harmonized.

Thomasino said every angel has its own language.

It was harmonizing. High pitched tones, not like ours. You could almost see the words and tunes floating out from the instruments. And I knew what they were saying. My Father must have given me the light to understand. It was just beautiful.

Did they speak about your mission?

Nope, they were just speaking about love, love, and love. What amazes me are the high pitched tones in different languages.

Were they all high pitched? All of them?

All high pitched, and yet, it wasn't like something you would get sick of. It was magnificent. There were no altos, nor sopranos, nor contraltos. It was all high pitched, but so beautiful. Something you have never heard here. And the Father and Jesus were present. And Michael was pretending he was the conductor. I said to my Father, "Look, look at him. He's supposed to be a warrior. Look what he's doing." My Father laughed. "**Michael had to get in it,** too," He said. And I saw Raphael, Gabriel, Hosches and Meleika. They looked at me with so much love.

They wanted to see if you were enjoying it?

They knew I was enjoying it. Then to top it off, my Father said how pleased He was at what I did for Mary for Mother's Day. He asked me, **"Would you like to see her?"** I said, "Of course, my Father, I would love to see her." And Mary came just like that. She had a beautiful rose. It wasn't yellow and it wasn't gold. It was hazel color. She just smiled, nodded and presented it to me. I could feel it going into my heart. I told her I would remember it always.

What did the rose symbolize?

Purity. It was a gift symbolizing purity. She gave it to me. And I said "I'm going to lock it away forever. I'll never forget it. I'll always see it in my mind." And she said, "I give you this grace, you will always see it before you." And she hugged me.

PART FOUR:
THE ROYAL PRIESTHOOD

18. THE DAY BEFORE THE ASCENSION
May 19, 1982

During her thanksgiving after communion, while she was with Jesus, Eileen had a beautiful relaxed smile. She did not respond to repeated requests to speak. When the Father joined them she spoke.

Why should I repeat everything? I feel like poll parrot..... **You must repeat.**

"I have my arms outstretched to receive them, but they will fall by the wayside. Eileen, I say unto you the hour has come. One more chance I give unto them. You must tell them this.

"I will speak to you, Eileen, through the wisdom of the Father. They will know these words come from Me, that you are but a vessel. I will warn them once again for this is the hour I am surely going to weed them. You will not frighten them, Child. You will tell them in simplicity and love. And they will feel this love, your love for their Father. It is not by chance that I have chosen you. You understand Me, Child."

I'll go wherever You want, but how will I know it's You, my Father? How will I know it's not just them wanting me to go there to socialize?..... You tell me to close myself in and to zipper myself up, and then You tell me to go. It's like a contradiction, my Father. What do You want from me?..... Will I know it's truly from You, my Father?.....

You know how much I like to be at home..... I just want to be lost in Your love, my Father. You are all I want, my Father. These things are not important to me..... **Because of my desire to stay** isolated, You find it fit for me to go out. If I desired to go out of my free will, You would pull me in like a fish..... Yes I remember. You would let it go faster and faster, and then You would rein it in..... When will You rein me in, my Father? Never let me go far..... I hope I am..... Father, I will do anything You say..... Nope, I'm not frightened..... Father, if nothing else, You have given me the grace to be aware of myself. I know what I am, my Father, and I know what I'm capable of doing and being.....

You know me, my Father, why do You ask me? I felt all Your tenderness and Your love and Your compassion. Your mercy and Your love for this Child made me cry, I guess. That's the only reason, Father. You know that...... No, I'm not afraid to step out, but I don't like being clobbered. I guess I lack humility..... I know they don't mean to..... We're all so full of self.....

I did?! You know I did, Father..... I try to remember everything You tell me..... You mean I forgot one?..... Oh, oh, I remember that. Father, do You really want me to go there?..... Well, I left it up to him..... What topic? You know I asked Him, Father, and he said as the Spirit moves me.....

But how do You do something like this, my Father?..... 'Course I trust in Him, I will trust in the Spirit..... Will it really flow to them as a steady stream?..... How will I open this?..... O Father, I can't pray in that way. Will they understand me?

"You will pray from your heart not caring who hears this, but the words will touch the depths of their souls. You will not put frosting on your prayers, nor make them elaborate, but always pray as a child to her Dad. This will open their hearts, and they'll be ready. For they will know a simple child of God has been placed before them, and His words will flow to their very souls. They will be touched and opened by grace to hear the message the Father brings to them through this His little one."

19. THE WORDS OF CONSECRATION
May 23, 1982

Jesus, the Father was trying to tell me something when I received You..... I know it's You. I hear Your voice. I feel·Your love. But the Father was trying to put something deeper into my very soul, Jesus..... I know it's You. I felt Your love. I felt Your warmth, and yet it was different from that, Jesus. It's something new from the Father..... I don't know how to explain it. You should know. You're there. You're coming to me. I don't know how to say it. It's like..... Well, I'm trying to say it. When I looked at the Host, I knew it was You because I listened closely to the priest's words of consecration. Yet I had a different feeling, Jesus. It was as if the word were there, and it was made flesh at the consecration, and it came to dwell in me forever at the communion.

I knew this before, but I could see the host turning into the word made flesh. And when I received, it was sinking into the depths of my soul, Jesus. I have always known that You are there. Do You understand me, Jesus?..... I'm so glad You do. I don't understand myself. I just felt it. I know You're there when Father says the words of consecration. And yet this was different. It was a new light on the word made flesh.....

Well, I meant it. I want to love You more than You've ever been loved, Jesus..... I want to love You more than You'll ever be loved..... If time ends tomorrow, or a million, billion years from now, I want to be the one that loves You best..... I know that, but I just want to be the one..... Thank you..... I'm always aware of Your presence. You know that..... (laughs) I call on You so many times, You need ear plugs.....

Yes, it's a good feeling, a sense of depth..... Well, like a new horizon. It's like veils passing away from You and the Father.....

Don't worry, my Friend, nothing will spoil me. How can you

spoil something that's not there?..... That's because You're You. You overlook all my faults..... I'll ask Him for sure. If You want to talk about it, it's all right..... Nope, I'm not afraid, Jesus, You'll be with me..... Yep, I'll stay with You, just loving You and being with You. But I can't shut them off altogether.....

Who told him to do that?..... You're going to have to do something with him, Jesus. He treats me as if I were a freak..... I know he doesn't mean it. He'll set me up to get clobbered, Jesus..... How many of them? Wow..... Makes me not want to go, huh?..... Of course I do, for the Father..... I don't know if that sounds so good or not, and I don't see why you're laughing about it. It makes me feel awful. You want me to change and You don't want me to change..... Oh, I don't feel very innocent. Sometimes I feel so cross, Jesus, I could almost choke him..... You know I wouldn't.... How does he know I'm going?..... Do you think she'll ask me?.....

What can I say, Jesus? Won't that be disrespectful?..... She didn't accept? You mean she didn't bite. Well, tell me what to say, so I'll know..... I'll tell her. When will she ask me?..... **Tuesday.....** **I'd prefer if Father didn't come. He gets me nervous.** That's all there is to it? OK..... No, I'll gladly say it. I'll not be lying. He does drive me nutty.....

Jesus, I'm really not happy about going. I know it's my Father's will, and I'll do anything He wants. But now that it's time to go, I really don't want to go..... Why do I have to tell Him? He knows everything. I don't want to upset Him..... Of course I'll do anything You want. I'll go for You and the Father.....

Jesus, what about Connecticut, is this what I should be doing?..... Well, I find peace in speaking what the Father wants me to speak. I don't find peace with people coming to me afterwards. For then they're talking to me, and I don't have anything to say of myself..... I know He will..... Of course I trust Him..... You have no idea..... Good, that's easy for You to say, You're a brain and I'm a dope..... You know I mean that truthfully. You know my heart..... Yes, I do and I am amazed..... For sure I do..... Jesus, I just want to do what my Father wants me to do. I don't want to do anything that I want to do. You know how I like to be home..... Thank You..... That depends on what You call showing off..... Sometimes I'm afraid I'll get speechless. Then I get a stomachache.....

Some of them are stupid like me. But some of them are priests, smart, Jesus..... **His wisdom.....** I just want to make sure they are the right doors, Jesus..... OK, I'll ask Him.....

"Remember always you are Mine and I am Yours. We belong to each other forever. When you stand, you'll stand tall and straight, and let them know by your countenance, by your love, that you are wed to me."

That's beautiful, Jesus. I'll never forget it..... **This is the only identification I need, my love for You. It'll show in my face, and I will draw them to the Father.** Thank You, Jesus, that gives me all the confidence in the world. No. I'm not afraid. Sometimes I might be a little, but then I trust. You always helped me. You're not going to let me down now.....

Thank you, my Father..... I want to do just what You want me to do. I want to say just what You want me to say, my Father. No more, no less. Father, You call me to do this, but I have such a craving, more than ever, to stay quiet in my own home. Father, why do I have this feeling when You call me to do other things?..... **It's an inspired feeling to stay home.....** I never looked at it like that..... Yes, I do understand. **There won't be any self in it because I will be going against my will.** Is that why You put this craving, this longing in my heart, Father, more than ever? **Then I'll know it's not of myself.....**

I don't know what You mean by doors, Father. All the doors?

"It's a very critical time for the Church, and you must go through any door your Father opens for you. You must speak His words to His people. Some will reject You, but only because they live in darkness. This is the hour of the Father. He's coming to His people to save the Church, for the Evil One himself is walking the earth to devour God's people. Eileen, he will strike out against you.

Stay close to the Son. His anger has been lifted against you. He stands in the shadows to strike out at his prey. But I am with you. Fear not, Child, for I am with you. I will open the doors and you will walk through them. You will carry My love to My people. He will knock you down and step on you, but I will lift you up. Go through the doors and speak to My people. Be not afraid, for you will speak in the Spirit. Your time is running short. You must do the Father's work. Go through the doors and speak to My people."

Father, I'm not the least bit afraid..... I understand my Father. But is it getting so terrible now?..... How can he have one foot in the door, my Father? This is sacred ground. It's Your Church, my Father..... Yes, I've noticed, my Father..... Whatever you want me to do. I just don't feel I'm capable of doing anything for You. I'll do anything You ask if I can..... I know, my Father..... No, I'm not upset by it. No, I want to be used by you, Father. Look at all You've done for me..... I love You, Father, I will do anything for You..... Of course I trust you. We have to work together and save this Church, my Father. I'll do anything for you, Father, by grace.....

I know, my Father. Don't feel sad. There are so many that love You so, Father. They really want to be good, Father. These will come through. Don't feel sad, my Father. You see, my Father, they must be hungry, and they're not getting the right food. We'll feed them, Father. They'll come back to You..... Don't worry, Father. Things will be all right. We'll do everything we can. I promise You, my Father..... Until my last breath. I promise You, my Father..... Don't think of them, Father. Think of all the beautiful ones that love You so much..... You tell me not to think negatively. Don't think about it, Father. We'll get them back.....

How many will be there, my Father?..... **Seven**. That's a lot. Well, I might worry at first, but I know You will say what You have to..... All right, I will, anything You want. I'll remember that my Father..... I know. Hosches will be there and Michael..... Father, could we do something. You know everything, and You know this is going to happen. Can You change it a little?..... I don't quite understand all this. If You know it's going to happen, and I can change it a little..... But You already know it's going to happen, Father..... It's hard to grasp..... I know. I learned that long ago, Father..... Would You want me to go there?..... Any door that You open. I promise. I promise You this, if You promise me You won't be worrying about them any more..... We don't want to talk about that stuff, Father. We'll talk about good stuff, OK?..... (laughs)..... Nope..... Loving You, loving Jesus. This is good stuff, Father. We know about those people, but we're going to work together, are we not, Father?.....

(laughs) It's big enough for sure..... Thank You, Father. I love You too, Father. And You know how much I mean it, Father. I love You. It touches my soul. I love You. I'm really Your child, right, Father? I'm really Your child..... I know I am. I feel it. I feel it so much. O Father, I want to make people love You. I want everyone to love You, Father.

INTERVIEW

He wants me to go wherever He sends me. He will send His Spirit upon me and I will speak exactly what He wants me to say. Because this is going to be a very bad year for the Church. He said the clergy and the people will take it from me rather than from the priests, because they know I am just an ordinary person. He said: **"Regardless of how you feel, you speak what My Spirit tells you to say and don't hesitate. You will know through the light of the Spirit what doors I want you to go through."** Capi is going to open doors that the Father doesn't want me to enter.

I told Him that He is calling me to do things, yet I have such a yearning to be in the peace of my home. He said: **"It will be a big effort for you to go through the doors that I open. But then you will rest assured that you are doing My will, and not delighting in this."** Then He said He wants me always to have this desire to be alone and not be up front. **"I'll know that when I put you there you can't wait to get back to your own home. I want you to have this desire to rush back to your solitude and quietness."**

He doesn't want me to have a craving to go out and be with people and talk. He said: **"I'm glad you want to stay home. Then when I put this desire in you to go through a door I open you will know it's from the Father."**

He did say Capi's going to be after me. He said he's raging, kicking up a big storm against me. He said he will show his colors through well-meaning people. I'm going to get clobbered again. He'll knock me down and step on me. He said, **"I'll put My hand out and lift you up again."** I'm used to that guy anyway. I get clobbered all the time. For no reason.

Oh, you know what He said about Father X. A lady called Father about my going to Connecticut and he's trying to get to go there. The Father said, **"She's going to ask you. You're going to say 'No' in a very nice way 'because he gets you nervous.' "** He said that wouldn't be disrespectful. He might go anyway. I'll just wait and see. She was excited about it. She called him and told him about it. He tried to invite himself. So she said she would inquire about it, because she's not in full control. My Father said, **"Don't encourage it."** He makes me feel funny. He wrote to the priests on the National Committee in Indiana telling them I'm coming. Out comes stupid Eileen who doesn't know what to say to them.

What did the Father say about that?

Not to let them get to me. **"You can meet them but don't linger with them."** They want to question me on different things. My Father said, **"Gracefully bow away from it."** The Father can put me in touch with whomever He wants. No one has to call up and tell them I'm coming. If the Father wants someone to cross my path, the Father will arrange it.

I know two of them. I don't know the others. The Father told me one's a layman, one's a Benedictine. My Father said he's alerted five of them. S. *[one of the St. John's prayer group team]* said, "Eileen, I can't wait to get you there to show you off to those big shots." Father X. got to S. too. They get me so upset.

See, Father wrote a letter and told of the healings and the knowledge *[word of knowledge]* and the tongues. They're going to look at me as if I were a dodo. The Father doesn't like this. And I don't want to be like a freak.

They'll want to know whether your gifts are genuine.

Oh, I don't mind that. But this is like a business deal. This is not being free in the Spirit. The Father will do what He wants to do. I don't mind Father R. I met him at our church.

My Father said this is a very bad year for the Church. He's very upset with His priests. He said, "**Eileen, they're leaving like flies.**" Isn't that awful? He wants to weed them out, but He feels sad about it, because He called them to their vocation. His heart was breaking and His eyes filled up. When His eyes fill up, His eyes get bluer than blue.

He said some are staying to try to turn the Church around. He said, "**Why, Eileen, they're saying that Jesus isn't on the altar.**" His eyes filled up again. He said: "**There is no getting away from it, Eileen, the Church is in a very bad state. The Church is in trouble.**" Capi is working with the priests under the pretense of a good spirit, and he's an evil spirit. My Father said they actually think they are justified in everything they do.

He said: "**Eileen, when you are standing there, you are not standing alone. You have the light of the Spirit. You will speak in strength from my Spirit.**" I said, "Father, I won't know what to say." He said: "**I'll tell you what to say. It's better you don't plan what you say. Not only do you have the light of the Spirit, but you have Jesus and Michael and Hosches. They'll be there.**" He said, "**What power is greater than the power of My love?**"

He wants me to be in peace and harmony. He said, "**Eileen, this is the way My children have to be.**" He said: "**Eileen, you know Capi can get in there and cause a lot of obstruction. He is knocking you down and stepping on you. He'll try his best to upset you before you go through one of these doors so You'll not be able to function in My light.**" I know what He means by that. I'll be paralyzed for sure.

You remember you read me something from an article by a theologian? He was turning Scripture around. [*This was a state-*

ment by a noted Scripture Professor, who said that the Scriptures are to be interpreted in exactly the same manner as any literary work.] You know what my Father said? He was the plaything of the devil. Isn't that awful?

He said many people will try to come and win my affections, not because there is anything different in me, but because they are looking for the supernatural. And He said, "**The supernatural is just loving the Father. You must give them this love for the Father.**"

Oh, you know what? When you were consecrating the host, it's as if the word came and settled on the paten. You spoke the word, you said the words of consecration and it floated to the host, it flowed into the host. When you gave me communion I could feel it in the depths of my soul. I could feel that word going inside me. As if the word were made flesh. I felt within me my Father saying, "**We'll give you the Word.**" He meant Jesus.

That word of the consecration went into the host and became Jesus.

That's just what it felt like. I knew my Father was teaching me something. My Father said once, "**You're priestly people, but you're not priests.**" He said, "**Eileen, you're not the priest.**"

NOTE: *Father X was an excellent priest of whom Eileen thought highly and of whom she was fond. He was understandably proud of Eileen's gifts and wished to bring them to the attention of others. This embarrassed her. He wanted to have a team ministry with Eileen. This was a praiseworthy desire, but it was not in the Father's plan.*

20. RELATING TO THE SPIRIT
Wednesday, June 2, 1982

I was delighted, Jesus. I admit I was afraid but You made up for it in the Eucharist..... No, she doesn't bother me. And all the love and peace You gave me took away that fear, that little upsetness. As soon as I was up there, I wasn't afraid any more, Jesus. I felt

You and the Father with me..... Well, yeah, of course, I'm going to trust for sure. If I didn't trust, I wouldn't go.....

No, Jesus, the Father hasn't told me yet..... I'm sure He will..... Well, I don't mind going a short distance, but I don't care to be away from home, Jesus. I'll do what the Father wants, but I really don't like being away from home.....

Of course I will. Anything He says. But I wish He'd use me around here..... Yeah, it was nice, Jesus. I was speaking to You there. I've seen it now. I really don't have to see it again..... Of course I knew You were there. Why do You ask me all this stuff when You're right there watching me?.....

No. It doesn't hurt that much..... You remember that? That was just this morning..... I don't know what brought it on. I think it was looking at all the green, Jesus. The life in the yard as I turned in and saw the beauty of the Father. I guess that made me a little sick, thinking I'm going to lose it. It won't be the same..... I know it will be better..... Well, for an instant I thought of the way it looked when it snowed, and I did feel sad, Jesus. I think it was because it was going to be taken away from me soon. That's the only reason I felt that way. Boy, You don't miss a trick! But it went by quickly. I forgot it, Jesus..... That's all right, You'll give me strength.

I felt sad when I thought of how it looked in the snow..... It's just humanness. That's a cop-out. I don't know why I felt so sad. But it left quickly..... Sometimes that pain does scare me, Jesus. I get so frightened. I don't know what's causing it.....

In a sense I'm delighted I can offer it up. But there's the humanness again, I get scared. It gets severe..... No, they don't understand. Let's talk about something else. Tomorrow night You're going to be with me, right?..... I don't know. The Father hasn't given it to me..... I thought of many things. I feel He wants me to speak churchy like. Let them know I'm a Roman Catholic, Jesus..... I'm not a theologian. I don't know how to put it across..... Yes, I depend on Him for sure. You know, Jesus, I figure the Father is going to have me do something, the way He was speaking to me this weekend.....

I don't care, so long as the Father wants me to do it.....
(laughs). Do I look that sad? I'm happy. That passed this morning.
It's gone by. I forgot it until You mentioned it.....

I know. That's why I want to do so much for Him..... I don't
know how short You call it, but I really do feel as if time were
running out. I can't put my finger on it, Jesus..... No, I really don't
mind. Of course I have ties, but I don't mind. As long as He uses
me the way He wants.....

(laughs) It is beautiful here..... I love the way Your hair blows.
It is almost as if the wind were kissing us..... Thank You, but You're
not the wind (laughs). But it's so beautiful, so peaceful..... There
You go, back to my yard. I said it was a fleeting thing. I'm not sad
any more. It just passed through my mind.

I know it's beautiful..... Thank You. If only they could see it,
Jesus. They wouldn't be sad at my leaving them to come here. I
wish You wouldn't keep everything such a secret..... But why me? I
don't deserve it, Jesus. I'm so aware of my nothingness..... I do feel
the Father's greatness.....

I know He does, Jesus. I love Him too..... Where? Isn't it
beautiful..... The most beautiful sight I have ever seen..... Look at
them..... They're beautiful. They look like our rabbits, but they are
not rabbits. Do You like our rabbits, Jesus? Aren't they cute? Did
You see them running around this morning when I reached for
one?..... (laughs) She did. She chased him right back in..... Almost
like comparing me to a rabbit..... Oh, thank You. Do You love
them?.....

He didn't tell me He was. I felt His presence..... Don't splash
me. I'm trying to talk to You..... I said I felt His presence. I didn't see
His face. But I knew He was there..... I know..... I think that's the
biggest singing in tongues *[at the Tuesday prayer meeting]* they've
ever done. I told them it was rising like incense..... **He loved it.** Aw,
You'd say that anyway.....

I know You do..... I just don't like You to be so serious with
me, Jesus. I'm almost afraid of what You're thinking..... I'm looking
into them..... Well, I see all the love You hold for me..... Deep

love..... I see You sense sorrow in me. I'm sorry, I thought it was gone..... Concern for me..... Am I attached to all these things?..... Well, if I didn't hurt, I guess I wouldn't have a chance to gain merit, would I, Jesus?.....

We'll ask Him..... You want to make a bet? I bet He won't tell me. What do You say?..... That's not a bet, You're agreeing with me! (laughing) Let's bet..... Well, don't gamble. Pretend You're not in Heaven. We'll make an earthly bet..... I betcha He won't tell me..... You have to bet different from me. How are we going to work this thing out?..... The trouble is You know too much..... Oh, that's no fun if we both say the same thing..... I can't change (laughing) because I know He isn't going to tell me..... You're not going to change because You know His mind.....

Don't let me fall in, Jesus..... I know I deserve it (laughing)..... I remember..... Oh, thank You..... I feel so good, Father..... We haven't been up to anything..... Talking..... Well, about the weather, about the prayer group..... Jesus, help me, about everything..... I wanted to make a bet about tomorrow night. I bet Jesus You wouldn't tell me about tomorrow night *[the subject of her talk]* and Jesus said, "**We can't gamble because this is Heaven, and gambling's not allowed.**"

I told Him it wasn't fair, because He knew everything, Father (laughs)..... We didn't come to any conclusion. We just came to You..... Well, I think You're not going to tell me, that's what (laughing)..... Thank You. I knew I was right..... No, I'm not afraid. I know You will give me something..... Oh, thank You, Father. All I want to do is to make You proud..... No, I should hope not. If I fall, You'll fall, for sure.....

Did You like it? I was very amazed..... Oh no, not at Your work, my Father, that never amazes me (laughs). Although You're always shocking me with something. I was amazed at all the voices. I know there were at least three or four more we could have had..... Thank You, my Father.....

I would rather not talk about her, Father..... No, no..... You know I wasn't happy with her. I really did feel a bad spirit, my Father. I just didn't want to upset the group when they asked me.....

Yes, I knew this for a long time, my Father..... No, I don't feel anything against her. You know me. You know the secrets of my heart..... I understand, my Father.

Nope, I'm not afraid. You'll either give it to me when I'm there, or I'll bump my nose. It doesn't matter..... I'll speak what You want me to speak..... He did? I thought You were strong on that doctrine bit..... I'm so glad, Father. I'm glad You were able to use me for him *[a priest attending the Tuesday prayer group for the first time].* Thank You..... How long do they expect me to talk, Father? Wow..... Boy, You better get busy. Write Your notes and read them to me..... Last night? How long was it?..... Really, Father? It seemed like just a second. We did well then, didn't we?.....

Nope, I trust You..... But he said it would be mixed. How mixed is mixed? Mixed Catholics, mixed charismatics, or mixed Protestant Catholics?..... (laughs) All of them. Oh boy. Let's not talk about it any more. I trust You. I trust You for sure..... More than anything in the whole world. Father, I love You so much..... Yeah, I guess it does hurt a little..... It's OK.....

For real, my Father?..... Well, what would he want me for, Father? He's so smart and I'm so dumb..... Yes, I know he's being persecuted *[a Bishop by his priests]*..... Yes, I know it's the priests..... Well, I knew some, but I didn't know how many, my Father..... Where will they go? He has to have some priests in his diocese..... How many left already?..... Did they leave the priesthood, Father?..... Well, what if the other Bishop is just as strict? They don't want discipline, they don't want doctrine, and they don't want tradition. They don't even want to acknowledge Jesus, because they'll have to change their lives, and they don't want to change..... Well, I don't quite understand the meaning of "free-lancer." Do what they want?..... But they can't. They have rules. What'll he do for priests, Father?.....

But he's made of good stuff..... If You want, I will, my Father..... Will they listen to me? They won't listen to him and I'm a nothing and he's a something..... I remember that. In my nothingness, I found the somethingness which is You, Father. How does that relate to this?..... I understand..... Nope, I'll do anything You want. Nope I'm not afraid. (laughs) How can I be afraid? Probably in my humanness—cop-out word—I do tremble. My knees knock, my teeth chatter and I get a stomachache..... Well, we'll set that aside. You're with me, Father..... Yes, I felt it. At one point I almost laughed. To think that stupid me was getting all that attention.....

Father, I don't know what I would do without the Spirit. Look at the rays. How does the Spirit understand me? I know by the glow He does when I speak about His love and my love for Him..... I don't see Him, my Father, as a person, and yet I know He understands me..... Look how bright the light is..... Father, why can't I see Him as a person, so I could love Him even more?..... Look at the radiance. How beautiful..... I feel the power. I feel the love of the Spirit this moment to overflowing, my Father. It's different from Your love and the love of Jesus. I can't quite put my finger on it. It's overwhelming right now.....

Is that what I did? **I acknowledged His wisdom**..... But it's true, Father. I could never understand without Him. Will I ever be able to relate to Him differently, Father? Like to You and Jesus?..... My toaster has power. When I plug it in, it has power. I don't love a toaster. When I turn the stove on, it's power. Father, I don't love the stove (laughs). But I love the Spirit. What draws me to Him like a magnet, my Father?..... It's a love, and yet, I can neither hug Him nor kiss Him, like Jesus or You, Father. Why do I feel such love for Him, especially right now?..... **Because I needed Him and I acknowledged I needed His light**..... I don't understand it all, Father. I see You. I see Jesus. I see light.

Spirit, I don't quite understand, but I know I love You. I know how desperately I need You, Holy Spirit. I know I need the wisdom and knowledge You give me. I need the light. And, Spirit, I need Your love. I can't be complete without it. I can see You as light and feel You as love and power. I don't see You as man, and yet I know You are there.....

Father, You can do all things. I feel Him overpowering me, Father..... I'm glad He's delighted, Father, I'm glad You're delighted,

Holy Spirit. I want to know more about You, Holy Spirit. I see Your work. I feel this love, this light. I want to know so much about You, Holy Spirit..... I relate to Jesus as my Spouse, and to my Father as my Dad. I relate to You, Spirit. I feel Your majesty, and yet I can't grasp it all. Help me, help me to grasp Your love.....

Is it truly special? I believe You, Father..... O Father, I don't hear His voice as I hear Your voice..... Yes, I feel that arrow penetrating the depths of my soul, and then I understand..... Father, I feel differently about the Spirit..... I never see You without the Spirit, Father.....

I do love You, Holy Spirit. I know I couldn't do anything without Your light, your wisdom. Yet it's not for this reason I love You..... I know He's important to me, Father..... Yes, I tell Him over and over. Holy Spirit, I see You in power and in light. I see You with my Father. I see You with Jesus, my Spouse. I can't fully grasp You..... I see You floating..... Father, I don't know what this feeling is. It's something different with the Spirit..... No, I'm not afraid of it. I'm delighted. But I just can't grasp it. Would You call this an awareness..... Well, give me a deeper word, Father.....

I'm with Him now. I am locked in with Him, Father. It's a wonderful feeling, Father..... I feel overwhelmed, Father. It's touching me deeply..... Thank You, Father. I love You beyond all understanding, my Father.....

21. CORPUS CHRISTI: THE LOVE OF JESUS
June 13, 1982

Yes I am happy..... I love You too..... Jesus, You look so beautiful today, so handsome, extra special..... Are You really in love?..... Yes, yes, for sure I am. More than ever. You are radiant. You seem to be glowing all over..... First You're a poet, and then a lover. I'll talk to the Father about You for sure..... Will they see it in me?..... Yes, that's right, they do see it.

[Eileen repeating Jesus' words]

"The fishes in the babbling brook know
that I want to love thee,
The birds in the trees know of My love for thee.
Turn not thy face from Me.
Let me press My lips upon thine,
Let me drink the love that I place in thy soul.
Yes, I want to love thee."

Jesus, You leave me speechless. I feel so special in Your presence. I don't know what You are drinking, but I love it. I love You so much, Jesus. I want so much to bring them closer to You, Jesus..... Is He really anxious? Look at Him, Jesus. He's beautiful. I get so softened up when I see Him. Do You feel that way, too, Jesus?..... I know. It's so hard to explain in words.

O Father, were You waiting long for us?..... O thank You..... I do feel radiant. I feel so good inside, my Father..... Yes, He has, more than ever, my Father..... Oh, it's **the love of Jesus in the Eucharist** [*today is Corpus Christi*]..... That's all right, Jesus, You can stay..... Thank You, Father, Your arms are strong, but gentle. There's no other place I'd rather be. I feel so safe, so secure.....

Yes, Father, I do love Him. More so today than ever. He seems so much more beautiful. Another veil has dropped. It's because of the Eucharist, He said. (laughing) I thought He was nipping at the wine..... I know now, Father, I know. The deep personal love we have for each other. I was just burning with love, a deeper love.....

But how can I tell them, how can I give them this love I feel?..... **It will radiate.....** Yes, I will repeat.

"When you speak of Jesus in the Eucharist to the people, they will know and they will feel the love radiating from you, and that there is something wonderful in the Eucharist. Not only by faith, but by experience. They will want more and more and more of Jesus. They will be drawn to the Mass, to the Eucharist. They will say, she's in contact with the Lord, and I want that too."

All from my face, Father? Not by words? I won't have to tell them anything at all?..... Yes, my Father, I do. It's not a case of wanting to be honest, for You know what I am. It's not that I have to tell You what's the truth..... At times I'm scared to death. How would You like it on Judgment Day, not knowing what to say to us. Do You have a paper? *[Eileen is referring to the fact that the Father wants her to speak without preparation.]*.....

No, Father. But what if You didn't know everything?..... That's the way I feel when I get up there *[to speak to the people]*. Won't You get nervous when it's my turn to come before You *[for Judgment]*? Well, that's how I feel.....

I keep telling You: it's ten minutes, it's five minutes *[before she is to speak]*. When I say we're going to be on in five minutes, You still don't pay attention..... Well, I trust You. It's not my fault if I get a stomachache, I'm scared..... I trust You. I have to trust You, there's no one else to trust.....

I know the Spirit's there. I trust You'll do it if You say so..... No, I won't back out of it..... Do You forget You're God?..... Because You're supposed to know all things. I do think sometimes You do forget You're God..... Nope..... That's what I'll do. I'll pray and I'll leave it all up to You..... (laughs) You don't have to ask me that twice. I love You and I adore You from the very depths of my soul.....

Am I really going to do that? That's all I want to do, Father. I want them all to know You and love You. I want them to be in the true Church. I want to bring them to You, Father..... You better get the Spirit to tap me on the head.....

INTERVIEW

All the love Jesus has been showering upon me in the Eucharist will radiate to His people. They won't know the deep intimate moments of this love, but they'll know I have something in this love of Jesus that they want. This will snare them into a deeper union with their God. Isn't this wonderful, Father?

16. THE PASSION. ORIGINAL SIN
June 17, 1982

No, there is no other reason. I just don't like to talk about the Passion. It makes me feel so sad. It makes my heart so full, so hurt..... Jesus, I don't want to talk about it.....

I know I should tell my director. Why don't You tell him? I don't like to talk about it.....

I'll do whatever You say, for sure. It makes me feel sad all over.....What gets me, how much You've gone through, and how much You loved.....

It's just too much to tell him..... I don't know if he could take it, Jesus..... Nope..... I certainly told him about the eyes..... What do You want, Jesus?..... You think it will make him love You more?.....

A book? I have a notebook...... Write this teaching? I'll write it..... Yeh, that's where I put all the good stuff. Why do You want me to put it into a book?..... **It's very important that man knows this.....** Tell the Spirit to make sure I get it all straight.....

You're the squeal, not me. I won't squeal anything. Jesus, can't we talk about something else?..... For sure, it's beautiful..... You could throw a rock and never hit the fish. Wouldn't that be a contradiction? If I throw a rock and hit the one that I am aiming at, how could that be a consequence of sin?..... **"Everything is guided by the Spirit, and here nothing can hurt anything..... Accidents are contradictions to God's will..... Here there are no contradictions. If you hit the fish, it would be an accident, and that couldn't happen here, because there's no sin here".....**

Jesus, is that why there's so much peace and harmony in this world, because the Spirit guides it? How come He doesn't guide our world?..... Don't You think that's Your and the Father's fault? You gave them the brains to do all this stuff and now they are doing it way out of proportion.....

I see..... The tree, too, is responding to love..... The flower is closed. You touch it open. It's responding to love..... Well, the Father said that everything in His creation responds to love, but I never connected it with the flowers and the trees. We have flowers and fish and trees. How come they don't respond to love?..... **Interference. There's no interference here**..... We'll ask Him together.

Father, I never knew original sin could touch everything..... Well, You gave them the brains to do it, why did You make them so intelligent?..... You knew this was going to happen..... Free will again..... But You knew it when You gave us the brains that we had the free will not to use them right..... Of course I do..... Why can't You tell everybody this, Father?..... But, can't You make them accept the grace?..... Free will again..... I promise I'll write it..... You're as bad as Jesus. What is this a writing contest tonight? You're both in cahoots about that book.....

Father X? He wouldn't..... He offered to conduct a healing service with me? What can I do, Father, a priest..... Oh gosh, oh my gosh..... Oh..... I think that might be easier..... That's such an awful predicament..... No, I can't do that..... Of course I feel like the last rose, wouldn't You? Why does he have to do these things to me..... I'll do just what you say..... No, I won't worry about it any more..... I'll be strong..... I know it's Your will.....

Yes, I remember the caterpillars..... It's just that it's hard for me to do this to a priest..... **I'm not doing it to a priest. I'm doing it to a service.** All right, I'll remember that. I will be strong. Everything is all right now. I'm strong. I'll do anything in the whole world for You. Even go through the fires of hell if You want me to.

INTERVIEW

Father X. is going to call me on the phone and say, "Eileen, I'll do the healing service with you." *[This is a teaching and healing service which Eileen was requested to give in Connecticut, her first. Unbeknownst to her, it was the forerunner of the monthly services she would give at St. John's Church, throughout the country and abroad.]* The Father said, "**No.**" The Father said he would foul it up. He said I should begin as He taught me, with a spiritual communion.

The Father said that in the spiritual communion, they are calling Jesus into their hearts and they are going to feel His presence, and they are going to know He's working. The Father said, "**Eileen, you're not bucking his priesthood, you are just bucking his interference. You can't let this happen.**"

The Father said I love animals and all God's creatures. He said the caterpillars had to be destroyed because they were not going along with God's plan. I squirmed, but I had to do it. *[A plague of caterpillars was destroying the trees in her area and throughout the state.]*

Jesus talked to you about the Passion?

I told Him I didn't like to talk to anybody about it, not even you. He said, "**Your spiritual director has to know. He's not going to tell anybody.**" I should write it all out for you. He said by knowing what Jesus suffered you'll have a greater love for Him.

On the cross, the minute the nail went through, His fingers came up into a claw like. And immediately the pain shoots up to His shoulder, and His heart feels as if it's going to break because the pain is so bad. Everything in His body twists so badly. The pain is so sharp, and everything becomes numb. The second nail is worse—He's all twisted inside. By that time the pain is traveling to the knees, the groin, everywhere. He was nauseated.

His tongue was so swollen in His mouth, and His lips so big and hard, puffy and He was choking, and so thirsty and so dry *[through loss of blood]*. No water can quench His thirst.

The thorns are sharp. And His eyeballs felt like monsters, and as if they were going to fall out. His head was throbbing, an awful feeling. Everything seemed to be out of whack.

He has a terrible pain throughout his body. The Father explained it. It seems as if the air stings with the slightest breeze. It's like putting salt on the wounds, everything is exposed. It's unbelievable.

As soon as the nail went in the feet the pain was so sharp. His head was like in a vise, as if pushed together. And He heard all the jeering. They cry "Crucify Him" — they hate Him. People, I don't know who they are, they hate Him. I can't see them all. A bunch of people hate Him and that feels awful, that hurts. There's no reason for them hating Him. They don't know Him. Not only was He being clobbered, but He was being hated. It's a different kind of a hatred, it's evil, vengeful, ungodly. And He was good to everybody.

When He was in the garden, his emptiness was a different kind of abandonment, a terrible feeling. Jesus's agony in the garden was not just rejection, but a pain of loss. It's a terrible thing to know you are going to go though this and no one cares. Some are going to love you, that's what makes it worthwhile, "**Father, OK.**" But He knew many are going to be lost anyway. And that's what hurt Him so much.

The Father doesn't say a word. He doesn't answer. Is He listening? Jesus didn't feel His presence. He doesn't do anything to console Him. He just watches. The abandonment is terrible. The pain of loss is worse than anything. I feel very sad and empty when I think or talk about it.

Is there anything else?

A lot. There is so much to tell you. I don't know where to begin.

23. FATHER'S DAY
June 20, 1982

Yes, of course I'm listening to You, Jesus..... Well, You're God, of course You know what I'm thinking. What are You asking me for?..... Oh, I just think everything looks more beautiful than ever today, Jesus. Even the air feels different. Or is it me?..... You can lift veils even in the valley?,.... Jesus, how many veils cover the valley? And how much beauty is hidden from me?..... Well, I would call it hidden. You're keeping it from me, aren't You?..... I guess that's a good idea, although I don't know how much more You could give me. Even the flowers look more beautiful than ever, and the stream seems clearer.....

Did I do something to let You lift this veil?..... The Father did?..... But I'm supposed to give Him gifts on Father's Day..... (laughs) I guess He does..... Yes, I remember the peace I felt as I knelt before Him. I couldn't express it to Him, Jesus. It's just as if the love were coming from my very soul. Deeper than ever..... Did He really?..... It brought tears to my eyes. I had to try to brush them away. Such a deep, deep love for Him..... No, I didn't realize that was another gift from the Father..... It was soft, and it was gentle, Jesus..... Thank you, Jesus.....

Will it last forever? Will it grow deeper?..... I felt it..... Yes, I know I'm privileged, Jesus. Jesus, I've never been so aware of my nothingness, but it does bring fear to me, sometimes..... Yes, I understand fear is not from the Father..... I can hardly separate them. I know my nothingness of myself, right, but I know I can do great things in Him by grace and acceptance to grace..... I've heard it over and over, Jesus.....

Is that mine to hold forever?..... Jesus, I feel awful. He's given me so much today, and it's His day..... Thank You, Jesus..... It sounds like such a long time..... Yes..... But I like to hear it.....

I didn't mean to offend You, I just looked in the mirror and saw how ugly I was, and it blew my mind that You would love me..... I didn't mean to offend Him..... Yes, I know He's created me, Jesus. But it's my face I see, I can't see my soul..... For sure I remember..... Yes, immediately I felt Your love. I won't do it again. I'm sorry. Do You forgive me, Jesus?..... I guess it's because I have such a low opinion of myself. I would never hurt the Father..... Yes, I know He's created me..... It was a weakness and I'm sorry. I'm truly sorry, Jesus..... If You say so..... Yes, I almost feel beautiful..... I will tell Him, Jesus..... That's right, if I reflect Him, how could I be ugly, He's so beautiful. I'll remember that, I promise..... Thank You, Jesus.....

I'm so glad He liked them..... No, I didn't tell anybody about them except the Father this morning..... And **He told everybody.**

Who's everybody?..... **Catherine, Dominic, Thomasino.....** For real?..... It does make me feel good..... We'll go together, hold my hand.

Father, I'm so happy that You like the present I gave You..... I thank You because I know I couldn't have brought it except by Your grace..... I'm fully aware I'm not capable of anything good, Father, except by Your grace and Your love..... Yes, I guess it was my free will..... That's what Jesus said, right, Jesus?..... But You move me to this love, my Father. Never have I loved anyone so much..... That's what moves me..... That's what Jesus was saying, the first..... Of course it makes me feel good all over..... It's wonderful, Father. I'm so glad when I please You.....

Yes..... If that's what You call beauty, I'm pleased..... I guess it's just because I felt so ugly at that moment. Jesus showed me where I was wrong, Father. Please forgive me..... I wish You would scold me sometime, Father. I know I deserve it..... I don't know. I'd probably feel chastised..... For sure I love Your way better. You never scold me, my Father..... I truly reflect You, Father?..... It's the greatest gift anyone could give me, my Father..... I promise I will do everything You ask me to do.....

Will You promise the Spirit will overshadow me?..... Thank You, Father. But You know the secrets of my heart. You know the feeling in my soul at this moment. Peace and love beyond all understanding, Father..... I'm listening well..... I knew it would be wonderful. I knew You had something planned..... No, I won't disappoint You. I need Your grace and Your help. I thank You for having such confidence in me, Father..... Thank You, Father, that delights me, for sure. This is always the best part of Father's Day, Father *[in His arms]*.

INTERVIEW

What was it about?

Oh, I looked in the mirror and I was disgusted with myself and I said, Eileen, you're so ugly and dumb and stupid. And as soon as I said that Jesus appeared and He said to me: "**Why are you doing this to yourself? Don't you know God created you? Are you insulting the Father for what He has made?**" I said, Jesus, I'm not insulting the Father, I'm insulting the way I look. I'm ugly and I'm dumb and I'm stupid. And He said, "**Eileen, what brought all this on?**" And I was a little snappy, I said, Well, You're God, find out.

When did this happen?

Yesterday morning. I was sick and disgusted with myself. And Jesus said I was making the Father unhappy by saying this.

He told you that?

Yes. And then today again He said: "**Don't you realize how you made the Father unhappy? He created you and He loves you just the way you are. Didn't He give you to me as My bride just the way you are? Did He change you overnight?**" And I said No. He said: "**Well, don't you realize I love you just the way you are? I like you to be aware that you can't do anything by yourself, but by grace you can do great things for the Father. You must say, by His grace I can do anything and I can be beautiful for Him and I can change. That is humility.**"

He said: "**Anyone who reflects the Father isn't ugly, because the Father isn't ugly, and you reflect the Father to your people. Sometimes pulling yourself down isn't humility, it can be an act of pride.**"

Yes. It is just disappointment that you're not the way you'd like to be.

Yes, for sure. My Father said that He loved me. He said: "**Eileen, I could change you into anything you wanted to be. A bird. I love you just the way you are. And I love the way you're advancing towards me and the way you try to love me and to please me. This is what's beautiful. Your soul is what counts.**" I said, but Father, I can't look at my soul, I have to look at that awful face.

What did He say to that?

He said, "**You reflect me, am I that awful to look at?**"

That was a good answer. He told you that you were the first?

Oh, I know. I was the first one of all the Saints and all the heavenly court who always prepared for almost two weeks to give the Father a Father's Day present on Father's Day. He said: **"They love me and they set out to please Me, but it's the first time I've ever had so many gifts on Father's Day."** Then He said, **"Maybe we're going to make it a legal holiday, Father God's Day."** I said, Gee, that'd be a good idea, Father.

He said, **"Eileen do you know how happy you made your Father?"** And Jesus said: **"He was so delighted, He talked about it all day long in Heaven to all the angels and Saints and the heavenly court, saying, 'Do you know what Eileen has done for me for Father's Day?' "** You know what I did, I wrote my name on a piece of paper. I put it over incense today and I burnt it. I said, Now, Father, Eileen's all gone and You're living in me. I'm going to move just for You from now on. I gave You myself, and now I'm completely devoted to You. Eileen's gone, she's gone up in smoke. He liked that.

What else did you do for Him?

Then I made Him a beautiful card, and I burnt it because I didn't want anyone to see it. And then all week I made little sacrifices and I gave it to Him all today in a big bundle and He can use it for any souls He wants. Then I took a whole bunch of flowers and decorated my room. I don't have a picture of Father God. I have the Holy Spirit, the Sacred Heart, and Jesus on the cross. So I decorated them all. I said, there You are, Father. And I made them all happy, the Sacred Heart, Jesus and the Holy Spirit. Even though Jesus is the Sacred Heart, I decorated them all, because I don't have a picture of the Father.

That's beautiful.

Jesus said that Catherine, Dominic and Thomasino were so delighted that I was inspired to do it. Jesus said they weren't the least bit jealous. They were just so overwhelmed that I did this for my Father. See, real good friends are like that. And Jesus said the Father was so delighted to hear me tell Father X to knock off giving way to this depression, get with it today, it's Father's Day.

The Father enjoyed Father's Day?

Jesus said that He was telling all the heavenly court, "**I look from one feast day to the next to see what she's up to.**" Isn't that beautiful? And I said, Jesus, He knows what's in my heart, and all its secrets. Jesus said: "**But you know, Eileen, you're giving all this to Him out of your free will. You don't have to do these things, but you give them out of your free will, and that's what just delights Him to pieces.**" Isn't that beautiful?

He has everything. He is the multiest, multiest millionaire in the whole world. He can make anything. And yet, He wants me with my free will to do these little loving gestures for Him. Doesn't that blow your mind? He waits for these little things that don't amount to a row of beans in a worldly sense. He is richer than rich. He's God. Everything is at His fingertips, and yet, He waits for my free will to move. Isn't that beautiful? I'm just delighted.

24. THE EUCHARIST AND PRAYER
June 23, 1982

Yes, I understand that well, Jesus..... You use that phrase over and over again..... I don't know how many. There's the Cursillo. There's the Charismatic movement. What about retreats?..... You're right..... Then why are they going to these things?..... Well, they go to share..... I can't truthfully say that I get nothing out of it. There's the Mass.....

You should have a consultation with the Father. He knows everything..... I don't know how I can make them swallow it. If You give them the grace and they don't accept it, what can I do..... Yes, I do emphasize it.....

Jesus, every time I come You lecture me about all this stuff. I know all this stuff. I don't know what I can do..... **Faith.** You've said enough about my going to Connecticut. Don't give me anything more to do..... I know that..... With my whole heart and soul I do..... If You say so, I believe You, but I can't see it in myself, Jesus..... I'll intercede. I love the Father and I love You so much..... I can see it's such a privilege to receive You in the Eucharist.....

See, all this stuff comes into our love-time, Jesus. We never used to have to talk about it before, why do we have to talk about it now?

Yes, so beautiful, this is what I like..... We don't like that stuff to come into our world..... Yes, I know, Jesus. That's why I like to come. Just You and I. We don't want to think about that stuff. It's bad enough I have to think about it afterwards.....

This is all beautiful for me. But will they grasp it, will they understand it, Jesus?..... Do they understand what is here? All pays homage to the Creator. Not because they have to, because they want to. They delight in it. Nothing grows old, and nothing is born. Nothing dies, and nothing is created..... it sounds a little bit dull.....

Nope, I don't find it dull. I find it exciting here. How can it always be exciting? Excitement comes and goes. How can it stay all the time and still be excitement?.....

(laughs) When these things come up I like You to clear them up for me..... No, I don't understand all of it, but I am curious. Now that stream's clear. Where is it going?..... Why?..... For sure?..... And it never gets bored and it never gets tired? It's hard for us to grasp..... No, I don't believe everything that's put before me, and I believe that's the Father's fault. He's the one who makes me look into everything and question things.....

If I know nothing else, I know that You love me..... I think it's because they never had an experience of the Lord, I really think that's what it is..... I find it so hard that they don't know and love the Eucharist.....

I think faith is always a gift..... I want to love You more than ever. I want so much for my people to love You, to realize that You are there in the Eucharist. I want them to love You so much. To love You, to prepare to receive You, not to take You for granted..... Yes, the people I speak to know that You are very alive to me.

Father, You know all things, You know how much I want to love You, I want to love You more than anybody..... Yes, my Father..... I need Your help so badly, Father. I can't function without You..... I need Your Spirit, Father..... Thank You..... I do, I sense Him. I know He's there..... Yes, Father..... Yes, I know what You expect of me, Father. I won't let You down, I promise You, my Father..... Thank You, Father. That gives me all the confidence in the world.

That's all I ever want, to do what You want me to do, to depend upon You..... Well, so peaceful..... I think it gets more difficult to leave You each time I am with You.

No, You're not letting me down, but let's face it, Father, You're God and I'm me..... Father You are God, my Father is God..... I am looking, Father. My Father is God..... My Father is God, My Father is God. I'm speaking to myself. My Father, You are so good-looking. All I see is God, God. I love you so much, God, God..... Father, I love You.....

INTERVIEW

Jesus was telling You that there is no love?

He said: "**From all the movements of the Church, Eileen, no love has sprung forth for the Father or the Son. The movements are gratifications. They are looking for something they want to find for themselves, but they are not looking for the love of God.**" He mentioned the Cursillo movement, the Charismatic movement, the people going on retreats. He said, "**Nine times out of ten, they are not looking for Me, they are looking for themselves.**" And I said, "So what's so bad about that?" And He said, "**Well, Eileen, they are not going to find themselves unless they find Me. Only in Me will they find themselves.**" And He brought to my mind that song I like so much, "Lose yourself in Me and You shall find yourself."

Jesus said: "**If they were looking for Me, Eileen — how many apostles did it take to change the world? Look at all the exploring. What have they found? Has the world changed? It's getting worse.**"

The ecumenical movement, the Scripture movement, the study of Scripture, He didn't mention them?

Once before Jesus told me, from studying scripture is coming confusion. He said: "**In the old Church, they can say what they like about it, the people got their Scripture from the pulpit, and they were better people. And you didn't have this confusion in the Church. Not that I want to keep My children in darkness, I want them to walk in the light, but the light of the Spirit, not the light of man, changing Scripture to suit their needs.**" Do You see what He's saying?

I think that the Scriptures should be studied, because study comes from God too, but I think we have to learn to unite study with prayer. And we have to recognize that we can push the study outside the tradition of the Church and its doctrine.

Yes. He wants us to be brilliant, He wants us to know Scripture, but not to distort it. He says He doesn't want us to be imbeciles, and be in darkness, but He says that the one who teaches Scripture should be founded and have his roots deep in Mother Church. It's essential that he should be a man of prayer. And that's the trouble. He wants us to accept Scripture as a child, without being childish.

Sometimes charismatic people know a little bit about the Bible and they're out teaching Scripture. They are not qualified. They are not theologians. Jesus is worried about this.

What about the Scripture professors who are teaching the seminarians?

The Pope wants Bishop Marshall to study the seminaries, to see the professors know their stuff. They are not led by the Spirit. You mentioned a great star. My Father said he's not led by the Holy Spirit, he's a plaything of Satan.

He was rejecting faith. Where was Jesus leading when He told you this?

More or less He was saying: "**Eileen, they are not all that they are cracked up to be, that they should be. I'm putting you, a lay person, out there. You are not educated in theology, nor in the doctrine and tradition of the Church. But you know what God expects from you. So when you go to these places, don't try to** catch up on Scripture or anything else. You say exactly what the Father says, and Scripture will come. Don't get hung up on what you are going to say."

There will be proofs. They'll know I'm not a theologian and I'm not educated in this stuff. They are going to take notice. They are going to take it from a lay person. They are going to know that it is the Spirit that's moving in me, not myself.

So He wants you to go through any door He opens, and you said it is enough to go through that door in Connecticut right now?

I have to go through that one. He said there will be other doors opening after this talk. He said it will be powerful and He said you trust in the Father. He will do the work and don't worry about it.

Then Jesus started teaching you.

He was teaching me that **in Heaven there's no death, there's no beginning, there's no end, there's always life.** I said: Well, how come you talk to me about excitement. Excitement has to have a beginning and an end to be excitement. He said, "**This whole world is a life of excitement and it will never end.**" I thought I might find it boring at some time. He said, "**Do you find the valley boring? Do you ever find Me boring?**" I said, "No, 'course not." He said, "**There are far more things for you here than you could ever imagine.**" Then He went into that whole thing: Look what the Father has planned for His people. I said, now You are throwing Scripture at me!

He picked a leaf?

He picked a leaf, and another leaf came. He took the leaf, and I said: "Now what are You going to do with this? You say nothing dies. What are You going to do with it now that You've got it?" He put it right back, and I said, "Is it floating?" He said, "**No, it's not floating. It's being absorbed into the same tree.**" I thought He'd crumble it and throw it away. He said, "**No, we don't do that here. We don't destroy.**" Everything has life, everything acknowledges the Creator. The trees bow to the Creator.

What about that stream, You asked Him where it is going?

He said it was going to the lake. I was wondering why it didn't become stagnant when it stopped. He said "**Nothing is stagnant here. Everything is alive. Everything is at its peak. Nothing dwindles.**"

He said, "**If these movements [in the Church] are all love, where is the fruit?**" He said, "**The faith dwindles.**" They're coming because it's the thing to do. Everyone thinks that marriage encounter is going to make the Church. They're getting divorces right and left when they come back from marriage encounter.

He said **the "in thing" is Jesus in the Eucharist.** And you get to Jesus in the Eucharist only by faith, and then you want to love Him. When you raised the Host, Father, I wanted to love Him—I ached. And that was grace. I wanted to love Him more than He has ever been loved before in the Eucharist. And I want people to love Him, not just by faith. It is good to love Him by faith, it's a grace. I want them to love Him in a personal encounter so they'll lay down their life for the Eucharist. So they can't wait to receive the Eucharist. This blows my mind. These people who are coming to hear me talk, this is good, but only if I can bring them closer to Jesus.

You gave the name of one of them and you said: Am I bringing her to You or to me? Why does she want to sit next to me, if I'm bringing her to You?

He said she wants people to see that she's next to Eileen. But that isn't what I want. It kills me. I want them to get back to Jesus. I know the Father is going to bring them to Jesus in a different way. He's going to use me for this. I don't know how. But He'll do it in His own way.

The spiritual communion is going to lead them close to Jesus?

I have a feeling that it is going to be fantastic. My Father is going to move powerfully because He wants to bring them back to spiritual communions when they can't receive. The "in thing" is Jesus.

You said each time you are there...

It's harder to come back.

And He said that came from Him?

Yep. And I felt more than ever, He's my Father, He's my Dad. That He's God. It meant so much to me that He is God. When you think about it—He's God. My Father, who kisses me and hugs me and loves me, He's my Dad, I can run to Him and tell Him anything, He's God. Think of it, it blows your mind! It means so much to me.

See, every once in a while I get a new light from the Holy Spirit. He's God, He's my Dad. It blows my mind, He was hugging me and pulling me so close to His chest, He's my Dad. I'm in the arms of God. So gentle, and light coming from His eyes, and more the more He looked at me. He smiled. The light was, He is God, Daddy God is hugging me, He's loving me, He's God, God. It blew me, He's my Dad, He loves **me**, me a nothing (laughs). It's tremendous. And the realization can only come from the Spirit. That's why I have such a tremendous love for the Spirit. You couldn't grasp this without Him.

Did He tell you anything about the Spirit?

He said the Spirit would come to me in a very powerful way, and not to worry about anything. He's in full control.

So you don't have to worry. When you open your mouth the words will come out. That's all you have to remember.

(laughs) Tomorrow I'll forget. I hope not. I have a feeling He's going to do something powerful about the Eucharist.

So please explain the teaching.

Sometimes at St. John's someone will get up to give a prophecy and say, "The Father is telling me a word, a blue word, and I just can't seem to tell you what it is." And then, "It's blue something. Has anybody got a thought about blue?" And the Father said to me, "**Eileen, when I'm talking to My children, if I have something to say, I will say it.**" Someone will get up and say, "I had a vision. I don't understand what it is." And the Father will say, "**If** that vision is for you, you will understand it, you will have the grace. If it's a dream, you can't believe dreams." I hear often, "There are many doors. Well, we could interpret that as the doors to the kingdom." The Father said, "**If I want to tell you something, if there is something behind that door, I will open it and allow you to see it. I don't play guessing games with you.**" Do you see what He is saying?

A man said, "I had a dream of a purple door." All I could think of was Veronica in New York *[Bayside]*, she's always seeing colors. I said to my Father, "Father I don't understand these colors, purple, blue, white, and black." He said, "**Eileen do you really believe I speak to my people this way?**" I said: "Father, You don't speak to me this way. But do you speak to the people in colors like this?" And He said, "**No, I don't.**"

I also get papers from a nun. She's a very good wonderful nun. But she believes fully in Veronica in New York. She's forever going to her shrine. And she sends me the paper. And all you see in it is colors, colors, colors. And the Father said, "**Why would I speak to you in colors?**" He spoke to the prophets in words.

A child flashed by you in a vision so fast that you couldn't see what it was. You asked Jesus or the Father to explain it to you. *[Eileen saw the face of a friend's grandchild. Afterwards, a fire occurred in the house.]*

It was a premonition. I warned her about it.

You didn't know who it was until the Father explained it to you. Usually it's a matter of praying for the person.

People who need prayer. I think I see them and start praying for them, and look back and it's not the person. Loads of people. *[She names a few.]* They don't have to be dead. My Father is alerting me to pray for them. The Father said: "**Tell the people never to stop praying. Someone will say, 'Well he's been dead fifty years, so he's surely in Heaven.' Never stop praying. Because from the beginning of time, I knew you were going to say all these prayers, so keep going. And if I don't use them for that soul, I'll apply them to another. No prayer is ever wasted.**"

You said that foreseeing the prayers, He may give them the grace before they die.

Yes, that's what He calls the grace of anticipation. Remember the truckdriver? So you can't say, "I don't have to pray." Of course we do. My Father knew from the beginning of time that I was going to say that rosary *[for the truckdriver killed in an accident, who said, 'My Jesus, mercy' as he died. Eileen said a rosary for him 4 hours later.]*

My Father said, "**Tell Maria, not to cry. Her father is with me in Heaven.**" He said it in Italian so I could tell her in Italian. I wouldn't have known how to say it to her. He is in Heaven yet every morning his name comes to me in the prayer for the dead. So the Father still wants me to pray for him. I pray for him all the time.

St. Thomas said we wouldn't know so much about Purgatory if it weren't for the poor souls appearing to people.

My Father once said it's their angel who appears. The Father wants prayers for that person. If we overpray, those prayers are not wasted. They go into a bank and the Father distributes them for the poor souls who don't get enough prayers. He can do anything He wants. No prayers are lost.

What happens in the case of a person who dies without having had a chance to be purified?

Who's to say he was not purified? You know what He's telling me now. He's telling me the parable of the two sons. The father spread out his table before him *[before the prodigal son on his return to his father.]* God will spread out His table before him *[who comes to Him]* at the last moment.

NOTE: *Eileen does not denying the existence of Purgatory. On the contrary she urges us never to cease praying for the deceased. True, in some cases these prayers may be anticipated and put to the credit of the person before they are said. She calls this "the grace of anticipation." Our Lady received the prerogative of the Immaculate Conception as a grace of anticipation — in anticipation of the merits Her Son gained on the cross.*

25. THE FATHER'S LOVING CONCERN
June 27, 1982

I didn't realize I was catching cold. I guess I was too hot..... Yeh, I do feel listless, Jesus..... Maybe it's the lack of sleep that brought it on — at least opened the door for it..... You're right..... Can I give it to You?..... No, that's one good thing about it..... In the morning it's worse, Jesus. Why are You asking me all this stuff? You're God. You know everything!.....

(laughs) You make me feel like a complainer. I don't want to complain. I'm not going to lose any merit with this one..... Maybe I spoke about my foot too much..... Thank You for saying that. It makes me feel better..... I know, they are not big crosses..... Father will give me the grace to take care of them..... Jesus, You know there's no need to worry about it.....

Yes, I was barefoot when I was watering the garden..... Jesus, I look as strong as an ox..... You're pampering me awful today. You know that don't You?..... I know You do. And I love You, and I like You to be concerned, but not to a point of worrying. I just want You to enjoy me and relax in my love. I promise to take better care.....

Uh-huh. Everything. Everything He wants me to do..... Yes, I know You do..... Well, I don't think You're scolding. I think You're concerned and You're loving..... I understand..... I thought I couldn't catch cold here..... You mean because I still have my humanness, if I walk through that water I could get sick?..... I thought there's no sickness here. You're contradicting Yourself, Jesus..... But I can't come here without my humanness. Make me spirit! You can do anything. Then I can go through the water..... Yes, I know it's a privilege. I realize that..... No, I don't want to ever do anything to contradict it.....

What will that do?..... **A deep, deep breath** (breathes deeply)..... **Again** (breathes deeply again)..... **And again.....** I don't know, soothing. (laughs) I could feel it going almost to my heels.....

I enjoy coming..... I enjoy so much my communion during the day, getting away from everything and everyone..... I know they'll be home..... I'll truly try, Jesus..... I know it's not that they want to, it's just that I'm there..... I guess it's my place for sure..... No, not to a point of distraction.....

Well, I don't know about that. I'm proud to be His child, I'll tell You, Jesus. I love the Father so much..... Well, I hope I do..... I'll try my best to make them understand how much He loves them..... I know He does..... I know He's there..... It does break my heart. But it will be all right, Jesus, more and more will come to Him. Maybe I haven't worked at it hard enough..... Yes, I will..... (laughs) He wants us to go over to Him.

Did You miss me, my Father?..... It's good to hear..... At least I try, Father..... Even that word kind of pains me to the core. "I try." I should be delighted, and You know I am..... No, it's all right. I don't mind it too much. I just don't like giving it to others, Father..... I understand, Father..... I'm truly sorry. I guess I more or less asked for it..... No, I thank You, my Father.....

Yes, He showed me how to breathe in (she takes a deep breath), and let it out, it feels as if something opens up..... Don't worry about me, my Father. I'm so used to these things.

You know I was so worried when that foot was getting better that I wouldn't have anything to offer. I was almost scared when it was getting better..... (laughs) No..... Only in the morning..... But I can take it..... I'm almost delighted when it does hurt, Father..... I was telling Jesus that maybe I shouldn't talk so much about the pain..... Oh no, not to everybody..... Yes, that's what Jesus said, he *[her director]* should know it..... I'm so afraid of wasting the grace..... This time I'll keep my mouth shut.....

Honest, my Father, I don't go looking for it, but I'm so happy when it hurts..... I don't know what I'm going to do when I have nothing to offer to You..... That isn't what I mean, Father. I mean, offering not the pains, but the merit and the graces so You can give them to someone that needs them..... (laughs) I love You too, Father.

Yes, I shouldn't sleep with the windows open.

INTERVIEW

Well the Father said I shouldn't sleep with the windows open. When I get very warm, I throw the sheet off, and then get cold when the wind blows in, and before I know it I have a cold. I didn't realize I caught it during the night. I can't stand the heat lately.

You feel that you are burning up?

It has been this way since I had surgery, and even in the winter I have no covers on, and the window is open.

So He was explaining to you how you got this cold. Then Jesus said that you went with bare feet outdoors, too.

Yep. I went onto the road with my bare feet. I was watering the garden with my bare feet. Then I took the hose and squirted them on my feet.

And then you didn't get any sleep.

He said I lacked sleep. The dogs kept me awake all the time.

Does the Father accept that, that the dogs keep you awake and you don't get any sleep?

He said: "**Be very firm, don't let one dog sneak up in the bed. Be firm. It will take a couple of days, Eileen, for them to get the message. They won't lose the room, they'll sleep on the floor.**"

So why don't you train them to do that? They interfere with your sleep.

I have to try. One of them wants me to love him continually. Pat, pat, pat. I brought him in so he wouldn't scratch the door. So he sticks his nose underneath me. I spank him and he cries.

26. "LET THE WHOLE WORLD KNOW"
July 4, 1982

Snap out of it, Jesus, I almost laughed and he'd think I'm crazy. You pull these tricks so often..... Of course it pleases me, but I don't want him to think I'm a looney bird..... Jesus, You're so cute. I'm glad to hear that..... Of course I'm filled with love. I'm delighted with what You did, but I just couldn't keep from laughing.....

You want the whole world to know. (laughing) I think there are other ways of letting them know, without them thinking I'm cuckoo..... (laughs) No, I'm not telling You how to run Your God business.....

No, You're silly..... (laughs) You dance better than the people in the world. Who taught You?..... (laughs) For sure..... **Together we will set the world on fire.....** Oh, thank You. I am too.....

What is that? It looks like a valley to me..... Mine? For sure?..... I'm just happy with my valley, I don't need that one..... Well, thank You..... If You give so much to me, how will there be room for everybody? I'm content with just the castle.....

(laughs) Jesus, yes, I take Your word for it. It is so beautiful. Is it really mine? For ever and ever?..... How come I haven't seen it before? Was it always there?..... You mean it was there and I just couldn't see it, and You revealed it to me now? Why couldn't I see it, Jesus? We've been all over this place..... This valley has veils too? You mean, it will get more and more beautiful here, as I draw closer to You, and when I come for good?..... Unbelievable! It's so beautiful..... Of course I'm happy, I just don't want You to run out of space.....

Of course I trust You. I love You. I'm delighted with it..... I see them, they look like ducks, but they are more like swans. But the colors, I don't understand.....

All right. Hold my hand because I don't want to slip..... That's right, **there are no accidents here.** Well, hold my hand anyway..... (laughing) No, I don't mistrust. I guess I do..... They're coming over to us. Jesus, look how clearly you can see them in the water..... Jesus, look at their heads, they lower them to You. It's beautiful..... Their eyes? Understanding, almost..... Acceptance..... Softness..... Love. That's what You wanted me to say, "love"..... Are You sure they will? They won't go away, they won't be tired waiting for me?.....

I just can't get over it. Look there. Tell me, how come? It's unbelievable. I was here and never saw it. O Jesus, You're so good to me..... Yes, I claim it. You gave it to me. I feel so selfish having it all..... It's so beautiful. I just can't believe it's mine. I'm very content with the valley, and the meadow, and my castle. I'd be content under a rock, as long as I'm here.

It's beautiful..... I can hardly wait. I don't think I could take much more, it's so beautiful..... Each time?..... Oh, thank You..... Yes, I remember that song, "She wears my ring to tell the world that she belongs to me. That I am hers and she is mine, for all eternity."..... Yes, I remember well. Thank You. Thank You so much..... No, of course not. I just don't want You to run out of space..... Well, there are so many people trying to get in. I don't want to be selfish and own all of this. But I'm delighted, for sure..... I'm really excited about it. It's just a new insight, Jesus..... No, there is never a dull moment in loving You..... I know there is more, sure I do. If You say so, I believe it, but of myself, I don't..... Thank You.....

Did He like it? Was He happy about it?..... See, You and the Father have secrets..... I guess we do..... But He knew from the beginning that You were going to give it to me..... He's really cute, huh, Jesus? I love the Father..... They're beautiful..... They're different, though. Even the animals are different here.

INTERVIEW

Tell me what the secret was.

Then it won't be a secret.

He gave you another valley in the valley.

Yes, you know, I was in that place a million times, and I never saw it. And it was there all the time.

And where did He take you when He showed you the valley?

There's a tree there that we play tag around sometimes. He took me behind the tree, and then another whole new valley was there.

Oh, right behind the tree?

Yeah, but I've been behind that tree, and there was nothing there before. And He said it is a veil lifted. It's unbelievable.

That's the secret?

Yes. Everything was so beautiful. There were like ducks in the water. And as we went down to the water, the ducks started swimming towards us, and then, when they got closer, I could see that they had long necks, like swans. But the colors weren't like our colors and they have feathers like ostrich feathers in a fan tail. I have a feather duster with beautiful colors, but I have never seen such colors in my life.

Even there?

Nope, they're different. And you know what they did? They looked up at Jesus, and they bowed before Him. Then He said to me, **"Look in their eyes."** I looked in their eyes, and I saw acknowledgment of the Lord and acknowledgment of me in their eyes. He said, **"What else do you see?"** I said, I see softness. I see gentleness. And He kept saying, **"What else?"** And I said, I know, I see love. They loved me, and they knew they belonged to me. Isn't that something? But the new valley is behind the tree.

What was behind the tree before?

Nothing. Land. The tree was a tree in the ground. We ran behind it many times, playing tag.

So, all of a sudden there's a valley behind there?

All this beauty, and it's mine. I'm afraid He's going to run out of space.

He can't run out of space. He has all the space He wants.

Not if He gives all this to me.

You know how big the universe is? He can make all the universes He wants to.

You know, Father, I've been behind that tree many times, and there was nothing. I said, but Jesus, I've been behind it. He said, **"I've lifted a veil. There is so much beauty you haven't seen."** I'm really excited over that. Then He threw His head back and laughed and He said, **"Eileen, you ain't seen nothin' yet, kid."**

Did He say that?

Yep, just like that. I said, Jesus, it's so beautiful. I've been behind that tree a hundred times. He got such a charge out of it. He

said the Father knew all about it and the Father was really excited
about my having it.

And it will be more beautiful each time?

Yes, the land will be more beautiful and there are many things
to see that I haven't seen. I thought I saw everything in my valley.
He said, "No." The valley and the meadows are beautiful, I just
love them. I can't imagine anything more beautiful than that
valley. And yet, He said, "**There is so much more. Just as the veils
fall between you and the Father, the veils are going to slip away on
your land.**" I'm not going to see it to its fullest until I'm there.

And in this new valley you said the animals and everything
are different? What are some of the differences. How about the
flowers, are they different?

They're far more beautiful. He's showing me different dimensions of the land. There's a lake, with these ducks, I called them.
And the trees are different. Everything's different. I know He's
going to show me more. I was just so excited.

At the very beginning You were upset with Jesus for something He was doing.

You know what it was, when I stooped over to get communion from your hand, it was Jesus giving me Himself. I didn't see
you, it was Jesus in your place and I started giggling.

I saw that.

Did you? Well, I started to giggle, and I said, Jesus, I know You
like to play jokes. He said: "**Well, I couldn't wait to come to you. I
wanted to take Father's place. I wanted you to see how anxious I
was to get to you.**" I said, Father will think I'm distracted and
giddy. If You do that in the church... (laughing) He said, "**Too bad
what they think. Too bad.**"

He's right.

Yes. But He took Your place and I started giggling.

Yes. Usually, you are looking at the Host. And this time you
were smiling.

I said, O Jesus, don't do that, he's going to think I'm distracted. And He said, "**Well, your director should know you by**

now." I said, That's what You think, I'm always a surprise to him. (laughing) Jesus said, **"Eileen, I can do anything I want."** So He changed into you, you into Him. He's also showing you the priest takes His place in giving communion. See what He's showing you. There's a serious part in it, too.

Is He telling you that now? What's He saying?

He just said now: **"See, Eileen, there are two sides to this. On one side there was my desire to come to you and to reveal Myself to you. But on the other side, remember, the priest is in Me, and I am in him. It is I that stand there."** There is this new teaching of the liberals. But see, He is there in the priest.

He said: **"See, Eileen, you believe this with all your heart and soul and you know for a fact that it is I. Now give this belief and this strength to My people. Let them know that it is I that live, move, and walk amongst them."**

Is He talking to you now? What is He saying to you?

"From your conviction, from your belief and your strength, they will know that I am moving amongst them."

That's what they need.

He says, **"I have placed you in this world as an apostle. Through the love that you hold for the Son and the love you hold for the Father, the world will know that God has revealed Himself to you. And you must reveal Him to the people."** That's beautiful, isn't it? All I can say is, Behold the handmaid, huh? Without God I'm nothing. Yes. He chose nothing to reveal Himself.

"In this nothingness," He said, **"I have found the love of my life."**

Then He said, **"We're going to set the whole world on fire with our love, you and I. And it's going to begin with this talk."**

NOTE: *The spiritual director has to be on his guard against confirming the beautiful things that God seems to say to the person directed, also against showing too much interest in them, lest he encourage a desire for the extraordinary, pride and illusion. In Eileen's case, she has been tested and her director is assured that she discerns God speaking to her. He is a witness to the fact that the extraordinarily*

*magnificent things Jesus and the Father say to her do not inflate her
with pride, but rather humble her. So it will be with this book.*

16. THE HOLY SPIRIT WILL SPEAK THROUGH EILEEN
July 7, 1982

Jesus, I enjoy it. Everything is just so right, just so perfect.....
Yes, I wish I could take a picture of it, and bring it home..... They
wouldn't be able to believe it, I guess..... Would I be able to take a
picture of it, Jesus?..... No, I didn't think so. I was just wondering.....
That would make a terrific picture of You, as You go down that
walk. Instead of the way they make You so funny looking..... No, I
don't think You are funny looking. I think You are beautiful..... I
don't think an artist could make a picture of You. They make You
so ugly, with strawberry hair (laughing).....

You are so beautiful. Why can't they capture this beauty?..... If
I described You, could an artist draw You?..... Well, I would
describe You as having soft eyes, hazel..... Nope, You're right, Jesus,
I couldn't really describe them.....

No, don't change the subject. I want to talk about You.....
Nope, You don't look like the Father..... You look like Mary.....
She's more delicate, but You look like her..... I don't think You take
after the Father..... You even have the gentleness of Mary. Father's
gentle too, Jesus..... **Not to everybody**..... That makes me feel
special for sure..... (laughs) Sometimes I don't feel so special.....

(softly) Yes, I know Him. I love the Father, Jesus, I truly love
the Father. With all my heart I love Him. I love You, too, but the
loves don't clash..... I love the Spirit. I can't explain my love for
Him though, Jesus. I love the Father, He's my Dad..... Right. I love
You, You're my Spouse. I can't explain this love for the Spirit,
Jesus..... Why do You ask?..... Well, as I said before, He gives me
light. I know it's coming from Him.....

Yes, like that novena I make to Him for the seven gifts
[published by the Holy Ghost Fathers, Wheaton, MD 20902]..... I
know He wants me to make it..... He puts it heavy on my heart..... I

just know how I need that novena, Jesus..... And I know I love Him. It's a different kind of love than for the Father, than for You. I can't survive without Him. Jesus.

I know He's a person, the third Person, but why isn't He a person like the Father and like You?..... Why can't He have a seat and two arms and two legs?..... Well, I don't think it would make me love Him more. I love Him just the way He is, but why doesn't He have all these things?..... But You said He comes from the Father and the Son, He's the third Person..... I don't see a person..... (laughs) I wouldn't love Him less..... I wouldn't love Him more..... I just love the majesty of His ways, and that light, and His power.

Can't You make Him a person that I can see?..... You know, Jesus, You take a lot for granted. It's awful hard for me to understand power..... Yes, I do feel it..... (laughs) I'm giving you a hard time today. I just wonder why You can't make Him a person. I don't see a person. I see power, I feel the majesty and the strength, but I don't see a person..... Nope, I know You made Him *[the Spirit proceeds from the Father and the Son]*. I know He gives me light...... Then why do I call Him a "He"? What if He's a "She"?..... (laughs) No. I just want to know what's going on.....

(laughs) Jesus, I'll ask the Father..... I'm not trying to be funny, Jesus, I just want to know..... (sighs) Oh, all right, I'll take Your word for it. But I'll come back again to it..... Yeh, I am stubborn. But I just like to know what's going on. I know He's strong, I know He's the third Person, I know I need Him, I know I love Him..... Him, all right, I don't like to call Him "it" anyway. (laughs)

(laughs) He's showing He's there, right?..... I do like You Holy Spirit..... I know You're here with Jesus, and I know You're with the Father..... It's just that You're a puzzle to me..... Yes, I understand the mystery.....

I feel that love, Jesus..... I know He loves me..... I feel that strength..... He's pleased..... Yes, Jesus, You do..... Is that why He surrounds You with the light?..... It's He who gives the light..... Is He just making Himself visible for me?..... I feel a deeper love for Him, Jesus, a deeper love than I've had before.....

Really, Jesus?..... Why me? More than the charismatic people?..... I feel Him..... I know I'm not very bright, and this wisdom comes from some place, and it's not from me..... I feel it in the novena. I feel the Spirit is pleased with me, and I don't know how to express it.....

Look at the way that light is pulsating..... Would You believe it, He wants me to understand..... But why is He such a mystery? Why can't You reveal Yourself as a person?..... **The Father's will.** Well sure, I buy that..... The light is pulsating again. The light is the Spirit..... And He surrounds the Father for sure because I've seen it, Jesus..... He's enthroning my heart in Himself..... There's life in that light..... There's power in that light, Jesus..... Where is He going?..... For sure I knew You're separate *[that is, really distinct]*, and You're in Him..... I don't see Him as a person, but He's there as a person, not visible to my eyes, but You and I say the Spirit is a person.....

It's pulsating again..... Only surrounding the Father and You..... I guess I'll have to be satisfied with that. Whether I like it or not..... Yes, He does, for sure He does, Jesus, You know He does, He's always coming through—in everything. He gives me just the right answers, His knowledge, whatever..... Of course I feel love for Him, You know I do, Jesus. I just can't quite understand how we could love the Spirit. It's just so hard to love an invisible person..... I do love Him..... For sure, it's a good teaching..... You know I accept the mystery, You can't blame me for digging into it..... Yes, I am satisfied with His love..... It's more than I deserve, I know.....

I love You, Spirit. I take You any way You want to come to me. I truly love You, and I know how much You help me..... I know I'd be nothing without You..... You give me the wisdom, the knowledge to speak. I know what a dumbhead I am. And I know how badly I need You..... This is the way You want it.....

(very long pause) The Spirit overshadows my soul. In this union He gives love and He gives light..... I feel His power, a new dimension of His love..... He will form and contain me. The Father wills it so..... I will find peace in His love and in His words. He will be my strength. He will speak through my voice. He will bring words of wisdom, of knowledge and of understanding to God's people through me.

I will walk in the light of day and I will find myself in God's love, the love for the divine Holy Spirit, a Lover that unites the Father and the Son closely. He will be my voice, my tongue, my hands and my feet, and I will walk through love knowing He lives within me. He will keep me on the straight path of righteousness and holiness. I will not waver in His love..... (long pause)

Wow, Jesus, I feel different..... Beautiful, light. I don't know how to explain it..... Thank You..... Yes, I do with all my heart..... I love Him more..... I thank the Father for Him..... Yes, I'm delighted with all these surprises You bring to me. I never know what to expect from You, Love..... Yes, I see how much You love me..... I'm anxious to see You, too. You've given me so much..... Yes, I know, I know You love me. I know that more and more every time I'm with You.....

(laughs) My director? The Father said to tell him every-thing..... Yes, I do for sure, but sometimes You work so fast with me, I just don't remember everything..... Oh, thank You..... Yes, I am truly graced with a special knowledge of the kingdom. I know I am, Jesus..... I'm delighted..... I can't convey this to man. They wouldn't understand me..... What day, Jesus?..... When I'm gone, gone where?..... Oh, here..... You'll have to tell him..... Oh..... Of course, I will. I understand. I'll tell him.....

Father, I've had the most wonderful experience, my Father. With the Holy Spirit..... Well, I'll tell You about it, but You already know! You're the Father..... The light was all around Jesus..... I saw the Spirit pulsating with love for me. I saw the light in majesty and power come between us. He was showing me that He was the third Person of the Trinity. I felt His love, I truly felt His love. I know He loves me, Father, and I know I can't survive without Him, my Father..... Is that wisdom?..... Thank You, my Father.....

Well, I just can't put my finger on it, Father, but it's a deep, deep love. A deep awareness that I need Him and that I have

Him and that He loves me. Yes, I am content, my Father..... I know,
I know, Father, and it blows my mind.

I know I don't deserve it, but I'm thrilled with the valley,
Father..... O Father, I love You, I love You so much, my Father. .....
I'm looking. I see the love..... My Father, You'll help me for sure?.....
Only to him. I promised Jesus only to him, Father..... Yes, he does
understand me..... Yes, my Father.....

I will listen carefully..... I will speak without fear..... You'll be
proud of me, I promise You, Father. All I want is for You to be
proud of me. I don't care what they think about me..... For sure I
will, I promise. (repeating) **"The keys of the kingdom He gives me,
and no man can take this from me. It is mine and mine alone to
have. It's a gift of my Father. The Spirit will protect me and the Son
will love me. I will hold these secrets as treasures within my soul.
Only when I am gone and free from this world of woe to be with
my Father, the world will know the kingdom has been revealed to
this little one."**..... Yes, Father.....

Interview

The Father just gave you a knowledge of the Holy Spirit and
the Holy Spirit gave you Himself in a special relation when He
overshadowed you, yes?

The Holy Spirit showed me a beautiful light all around Jesus
and when I told Jesus how much I loved the Spirit, the light
pulsated. That's the first time I saw the light pulsating. And then
the light went from Jesus, and it was over here *[approaching
Eileen]*. It was magnificent. It was powerful, but without arms, legs,
head, or body. He was showing me He is a separate person. I have
seen the light around the Father and around Jesus.

You know, if there is an intelligent being that loves, that is a
person, even though there is no body. An angel is a person.

He loves me for sure.

He gave you a special gift this time.

A deeper love, it is a special relationship, almost like a nuptial relationship. A control, a complete control of me. I belong to Him. My mind, my thoughts.

Did you get the light from Him that it was a nuptial relationship?

Like a nuptial relationship, but not like Jesus' nuptial, and not like the relationship with my Father. The Spirit is in control of my mind, my soul. I felt He is going to function through me, **"If you want me to,"** He's not forceful, **"I will function through you, I will speak words through you, I will speak wisdom and knowledge through you."**

That's a special relationship.

He came inside of me as a cone of light, and I felt a deep, deep love, a deep peace, not overpowering. I know without a doubt now He's going to speak powerfully through me.

And that relieves you of your fears about speaking?

Yes, He's going to speak. He's in control. He's going to speak powerfully through me because I love Him. He is going to do it. I'm one with Him, I'm united with Him, do you understand?

Beautiful.

A deep peace, a deep love. I'm not afraid of anything.

And the Father was pleased with that?

The Father was delighted.

The Father said it was a present from both Jesus and the Father?

The Father said, **"Now you are in love w   Him."** And He knew I was. **"When you want to speak, the   ￼irit will speak through you. He'll give you the spirit, He'll give you the keys, and He'll give you the courage, He'll give you the wisdom and the knowledge of anything you have to do. He's My office within you."**

[Note: Here the Father explains what He means by "the keys" given to Eileen. They have nothing to do with the keys of Peter, the power to bind and loose given to the hierarchy.]

He's always with you?

In a very special way?

In a different way. I knew He was always there because I could understand things and I know I'm not bright. But this is different, this is different.

He has taken possession of you?

Yeh. He's in me. We're one. He's going to function through me. (gasps) **He's going to use my eyes, my tongue, my hands and my feet. He will function. Like I am a shell and He's taken over.**

His grace is coming to you, He has Eileen to use?

I don't know. I'm not so great. I know I'm not a saint. But I'm powerful in the Spirit. I know He's going to do things. You know what comes to me, "I live, now not I, but He lives in me." Eileen's a dumbhead, but with the Spirit in me, I can be smart, and I can be powerful, and I can give the Father's message. And people will listen to it, because the Spirit is speaking through me. Because He's within me, He's dwelling in my soul. He took possession of my being, because I want Him to. He didn't force it, I want Him to.

Are you satisfied that you don't see Him in a body?

I don't know. I'd like to know what He looks like. He says: "**I look like power and mystery and light and knowledge, I am part of your life. Accept Me as I am.**" I accept Him.

And what did the Father say about your director?

My Father and Jesus say I must tell you all of this and I've done it, but I mustn't tell anybody else. They are not going to have the grace to understand it. But when I go, they will understand it.

You asked the Father how they are going to understand it when you are gone. What did He say?

"**Your director will reveal what has to be revealed about you. Don't let this bother you.**" I'm not bothered by it. I was just bothered because He said, "They'll know about you when you go." I wondered, "Who's going to tell them?" He said you.

NOTE: *These events and words explain the spiritual fruitfulness of Eileen's teaching and healing services given throughout the United States and abroad. See* Eileen George:Beacon of God's Love:Her Teaching, *1990.*

28. JESUS WILL NOT BE SO AVAILABLE IN THE EUCHARIST
July 25, 1982

Eileen sees people running after the Host, but they are unable to reach It. The Host heads for the Father's heart. She asks what this means. Jesus explains that He is not going to be so available for people in the Eucharist in the future. Eileen says there will always be a priest in the parish. Jesus says not to count on it. Jesus is returning to the Father. Why?

People lack a genuine devotion to the Eucharist, the devotion she has. Eileen tries to excuse them: He has treated her differently since she was a child; He can't expect them to feel towards Him the same way she does. He says she is shifting the blame. She replies she doesn't know whom to blame. Maybe herself. "I'm not a good example. I try, but not enough, so I could take the blame." She continues to excuse the people: many of them have not been taught. Jesus asks her to pray for His priests.

He tells her that priests will come to her from all parts of the country. He wants her to teach them that He is present in the tabernacle.

7. Monsignor Hugh Nolan, Ph.D., editor of the U.S. Bishops Pastoral Letters, and Eileen

8. Eileen with her private chaplain, Father Augustine Esposito, OSA

9. Father Norbert Weber, Pastor of Holy Family Church, Nazareth, Penn., and Eileen, March 1992

10. Eileen with diocesan priests to whom she has given a conference, Watertown, N.Y., June 1992

11. Eileen with Augustinian Priests after a Priests Conference, St. Mary's Church, Lawrence, Mass

12. Franciscan Seminarians with Eileen and Father Augustine Esposito, OSA

PART FIVE:
THE VALLEY

29. A SAINT WILL COME WHEN DESIRED
May 19, 1982

I didn't know it was visible. I don't want to bring my worries here, Jesus..... But you know everything. You know what it's about..... I know You have so many worries. I don't want to give You any more. I don't want to talk about it.....

Well, You know how much love the Father has put in my heart for the priests, Jesus..... Look at that article in the paper this morning. I don't think they should have put it in the paper with his picture, and his wife and children..... If he wants to get away from the priesthood, why does he have to advertise it?..... I'm sure Capi had his hand in it.....

Well, yes, even that one with his child. Does he have to tell everybody he was a priest and now he's married?..... I imagine Capi works that way. But why are we giving him a free hand? If they want to leave, why don't they just do it silently and stay in the background, why do they have to project themselves? This is what has been disturbing me, Jesus.....

Yes, I understand. I don't want to bring these troubles into this world, Jesus. I want to have peace and love here..... Well, if You want to talk about it. I'm not bringing it up, You are the one..... Yes, I know the priesthood is a great mystery, and I love it, Jesus. I truly love the priesthood..... Yes, I'll do whatever the Father wants.....

Yes, I remember that..... He said he would strike at the heart of the Father, the priests. I just don't like to bother You..... Well, maybe **I am working with a grown-up**..... Nope, I don't like to bring them into our world..... 'Course I love You, more than anything in the whole world.....

Yes, **You're the High Priest.**..... Yes, I understand that..... But You're God, You know what's going on, why do I have to tell You?..... Does it make it easier when I say it?..... I'm not hiding it. I know I can't hide anything from You..... For sure..... But do they know You're the High Priest? Do they really know it, Jesus? Do they truly understand this mystery?.....

It's not really a mystery...... You're right, the mystery is the Trinity, it goes even deeper. **You gave them truth and gave them proof.**..... Then they should grasp it, right?..... For sure..... They truly don't let the High Priest take over. Else they wouldn't act like this. I'm sure they wouldn't, Jesus..... Yes, **they are instruments of grace.**.....

It bothered me all during breakfast. It bothered me during the morning. I don't think they should have advertised it in the paper as they did..... Yes, **some are striking out at the Church, under the pretext of good.**.....

I'm sure they will know that I love them..... (laughs) Love is different with God..... Thank you..... Yes, I will, anything You wish. I'm delighted, it's as if I have a secret..... What tape?..... (laughs) Oh, of my talk?..... Well I'm tired of all this shop talk..... I know it's necessary.

Do the ducks in the water know we are here?..... Jesus, how is it You don't let people come here when I'm here?..... No, I'm not changing the subject. I just want to stop the shop talk, I guess..... (laughs) How is it You don't let people come when I'm here?..... Well, all the people. The same ones that come to a party or celebration, how come they don't even walk by, how come I'm so isolated?.....

How would You do that?..... Well, OK, Benedict, because it's his feast day..... There he is. You mean that's all I have to do, desire them, and they'll be present to me?..... And all this time I've been alone because I haven't been desiring them?..... Oh, **they won't invade my silence and solitude. They come just when I wish them to be here.**..... Will it be like that when I'm here forever?..... **They'll come only when I ask them to. It's freedom. I can choose to be** alone, if I wish, and choose to have company when I wish. But if they don't choose to be with me? Won't I be invading their freedom?..... Is there that much love? Well, I know there is, but I just can't grasp that much. Maybe I'll be able to grasp it when I'm here forever..... (laughs) He's by the water. You're the one who asked me to wish, to desire..... He's coming towards us.....

Hi, Benedict. You know why you're here?..... (laughs) How did you know I desired you?..... I'll be honest with you, Jesus told me to think of somebody I wanted to see, and you came to my mind..... I didn't have anything I wanted to talk about. Well, maybe I do. Benedict, what are you going to do with the monastery? Are you going to let it run its course or are you going to take action, Benedict?.....

They won't listen to me. You know it, Benedict, why ask me?..... I don't know. Benedict, what are we going to do?..... No, I wouldn't want that to happen. We have to think about everybody..... Ask the Father..... I understand the free will..... I know..... Well, between you and the Father and Jesus, you better come up with something.....

You are a good listener, but you are not opening your mouth to help us..... Well, you could talk to them..... I don't know much of anything, but I know the Father wants a good monastery, Benedict. Couldn't you do something for them today?..... Ask the Spirit to come in a special way in your honor..... I know..... Obedience, humility, submission — that's a powerful sweep, I'll tell you..... Right, I'll pray for sure.....

Stop, stay for a while and tell me some more..... What?..... Please don't go..... Well, you're not burdening me. I guess I know most of this stuff..... Nope, you'll never bother me, for sure.....

Well, I'll never let them get to me, I promise you, Benedict. You know I won't..... I promise I will..... Well, yes, he asked my friend to bring me up there to speak with him..... No, I wouldn't go, you know I wouldn't. That's the furthest thing from my mind, Benedict..... I'm not impressed. It just doesn't seem right to me, Benedict..... Well, yes, I have a good insight into monastic values.

Between you, Thomasino, Doctor Mellifluous, I learned quite a bit.....

Yes, I would like to go to Him, Benedict. I love Him, and I thank you..... For sure, I will..... Yes, I see Him. Thank you again. Come back, please. I love you.

No, Father..... I'm glad You came..... I was talking to Benedict..... About little problems, my Father. Nothing I want to bother You with..... Well, You know them already. Only we won't talk about them, OK?..... Let's talk about happy things..... Well, I was telling Jesus that I'm finding so much peace, and that's since the Spirit came into me, my Father, in such a special way. I'm completely relaxed, my Father.....

To be with You, Father, to look into Your eyes, I just want to be with You..... I know, but it's a different kind of a union. You know what I mean, You're Father God..... I know but it's far deeper than that. You know what it is, I just can't express it.....

It's a terrible wound, Father. You put this desire to share in my heart..... I'd like to give it to them if I can. It depends upon the Spirit, Father..... I thank You, Father. I will remember that, **they will know that I walk with my Father.....**

30. THE BEAUTY OF THE VALLEY
July 28, 1982

I'm just taking in all the beauty. It's so peaceful here. I don't ever want to leave it. Everything is so quiet, Jesus..... No, I have never seen such beauty. Everything seems to complement everything. Look at those hills, the way they complement the sky. The grass. The colors are so different. They complement each other.....

Yes, I notice that. There's a peaceful air about them, as if they know they are in a special place. The flowers know they should be here. They're in a place of peace and happiness. No sin, no frustration. O Jesus, everything is different here..... 'Course it does. It makes you want to stay here forever.

Yes, I do get tired of the hustle and bustle of the world..... I get tired of everything lately..... No it's not for me to say. (laughing) I'll come when the Father calls me..... No, I wouldn't tell Him that. It's up to Him. You know my faults, how imperfect I am, Jesus. As much as I'd like to be here, I just have to get rid of these things, this bunch of junk. Don't you want me to be more pleasing to You?..... (laughs) No, He didn't say it, but I know what I do..... No, I don't want You to speak to the Father..... (laughing) He'll do it in His own time......

Oh, thank You..... Look at the stream that runs so gently, Jesus..... I do, I do. When I get so tired I do that. You know I do. I try to close my eyes and grasp all this beauty and peace and block out everything..... Yes, I guess I am yearning for it more..... I don't know. I think the Father puts this feeling in my heart to get things in order. Then He'll come. I can't say whether today or tomorrow. But it sounds close to me.....

I separated his winter clothes and got them all cleaned this fall for school..... Nope, not at all. Well, sometimes, maybe a little..... I don't know. I can't express it..... Well, as if I am going on a trip, and I want them to have everything that will make them comfortable *[while I am gone]*.

31. MARY AT THE PINNACLE OF LOVE
August 1, 1982

I'm excited watching them. I know it's not new to me. But I'm wondering why you invited them..... No, I love to watch them. They go so gracefully through space. They don't touch the ground.....

They're making a garland..... They know it's going to be my place. Who invited them?..... I'm delighted. Look at them, how beautiful they are. How is it they can see me? Yet when you take me to other places, they can't see me..... Oh, **this is my place**, Jesus. Well the other places, the dimensions of Heaven, they couldn't see me, don't you remember?..... (laughs) I knew You'd remember.

They can see me because it's my castle, it's my valley, and it's the place that I'm going to be. You and the Father will it so. In the other plateaus they're not allowed to see me, because I'm not of their world yet. But I could see them..... No, **I couldn't touch them.....** It's as if my hand went through them, Jesus. **I can't touch these either.....** Well, how come Thomasino hugged me and I felt his hug? He touched me, and I felt him..... You mean if I reached out I couldn't touch him?..... Well, (sighs) it's confusing to me.....

(laughs) Look at them. Aren't they beautiful? I have never seen such beauty...... **It's their love. They radiate love. It's a beauty that surpasses all earthly beauty.** Yes, I can buy that, for sure..... Jesus, when I'm here will they come to visit me often..... Oh, thank You. I think you're trying to bribe me to come faster. You better speak to the Father..... It's so beautiful..... I'm just so happy..... They want us to go with them. Don't go too fast.....

What is the garland called? Does "garland" mean the same as our garlands?..... (laughs) Well, because everything is so different here, I have to ask..... No, I'm not writing a book, (laughs) I just want to remember. I have a hard time remembering everything. Well, tell the Spirit to snap it up, then I won't forget.....

(laughs) Look what they're doing. They walk right over the water..... It's beautiful. It's hard to imagine a place that's always happy — with real genuine happiness I mean. Not for a minute —forever. Never tiring of it. Always enjoying it..... I think You're just trying to tempt me, Jesus!..... That's what You think. I know better than to tinker around with the Father.....

'Course He does. If I know nothing else, I know the Father loves me..... (laughs) See, she is coming. Well thank You, it's so beautiful. You have one too, Jesus. (laughs) The Bobbsey twins..... Thank you so much..... They don't speak, and yet I hear..... Maybe if You did that to us on earth, we wouldn't get into all these messes. (sighs)

Come, let's go sit with them..... No, I don't want to take it off and put it in the stream. You'll hurt their feelings. Here, take these other ones. Hey, You're God, You're not supposed to hurt feelings.

I'm not supposed to have to tell You..... (laughs) I love to hear You laugh like that.

Jesus, how is it You don't laugh *[in representations]?* You look like an old grouch all the time. You look so somber..... **The artist's conception of You.....** Well, can't You give one the thought of having You laughing and smiling?..... **Your love. (laughs)** Thank You.

Sure it thrills me. I get so excited about it. It blows my mind..... You know I pray for that. That everybody know You like I know You. And yet I have a little bit of self-centeredness. I don't want anybody to know You as much as I know You. Is that awful?..... (laughs) Thank you.....

Yes, I noticed that in my talk. Would it be kosher to do this, Jesus? Would I be stepping out of line?..... Well, I mean, I'm a Roman Catholic. Eucharist is Eucharist..... I guess You're right, it is cold. It's almost like being a soldier...... I can't say "Jesus." "Eucharist gives you Jesus." That does have a softness about it. "Eucharist gives you Jesus." "Eucharist is the Eucharist, and gives you Eucharist." "Eucharist gives you Jesus." There is a difference, Jesus. I know what you mean. "The priest gives you Jesus." "I'm going to Jesus," not "I'm going to Eucharist." A softness. I'll remember. I promise you. Yes, it's like a different kind of relationship.

Eucharist is Eucharist. But being human, "I'm going to Jesus" is more meaningful, more intimate. And it's all right to say that? Me a nothing, I'm going to Jesus. That sounds great, Jesus. I will make a tape about it. Thank you. I was wondering if I was making too many tapes.....

(laughs) First you tell me to come. Then you tell me to stick around and make tapes. You better make up your mind, Jesus..... Yes, I will. I'll title it "I'm Going to Jesus." That sounds super. See how you teach me?..... (laughs) Well, I'm not tired yet, just keep it up and I might be.....

Look what they're bringing us..... I thank you..... What is it?..... **It's nectar, from the center, the heart of the flower. It does not drain the flower.** It revives my soul. And this will go on for all eternity.....

It's delightful. Sweeter than sweet. I learned so much, Jesus. I just hate to go back. Nectar from the center of the flower and it revives my soul. It's refreshing. It's a taste beyond sweetness..... It's been given to me by the angels. Would you call it a love potion?..... (laughs) How else can I title it?..... That's very beautiful. **From the center called the heart of the flower, the angels have taken the nectar and given it to me.** It tastes so sweet, a sweetness beyond all sweetness.

The delicacy of my God. I taste and see how sweet Thou art. And though unspoken I know it revives my soul. It fills me with delight and love. I feel refreshed anew, and yet, it's just a beginning of the delights and of the secrets that my Savior has prepared for me. Oh my Love, my soul cries out to thee, can I stand much more..... Yes, Love, I feel revived, I feel light. I feel not blood, but love flowing through me. I don't understand, and yet I do.....

Love, is it You? I know not what to say. From the center of the flower comes this drink given to me by the angels. Drink, my Beloved and cling to me. You have gone into ecstasy, where no man can touch You, just me, just me, my Love, just me..... (long pause)

Jesus, just for a split second, I felt a new awakening ..... Such beauty, it blows my mind. A new awareness of Thy presence ..... What have you put in this cup, my Love?

My eyes are deceiving me. Can one place hold so much beauty?..... No, I just stand in awe. It's so hard to grasp..... The different Heavens. It's unbelievable. A part of Scripture jumps out at me, Jesus. "No eyes have seen, no lips have spoken, no ears have heard the glory that He has prepared for thee." I feel lightheaded, almost intoxicated, Love. Could I be dreaming? I'm climbing higher and higher, as I climb the beauty is so breathtaking. There's more. There's more. I don't want to stay below any longer. I want to go higher. Father's presence is greater. Your love seems deeper. Now no earthly thing will pull me down..... If I do not see Him, my heart will burst, Jesus. Where is He?..... My Father, where are

You?..... Father, why can't You reveal this to man?..... What do You mean, my Father? **No man has ever been allowed to see so much.**

But where is the pinnacle of Your love?..... Mary! The pinnacle of love is love. She sits in splendor, in beauty and in innocence. And yet I call her Mother..... She's beckoning me to come. **Come beside me.....** (long pause) She cradles me in her arms. I belong here. And though it is Mary's arms, I feel my Father, though at this moment I see Him not. It's all in one and one in all, and I belong. I belong..... Yes, Mother..... Your voice falls upon my soul as gentle morning dew. The thirst I feel is over..... Yes, I'll come to you soon..... Yes I will, yes, my Mother..... I'll never forget, never, though the ray of the sun passes, I'll never forget, I'll never forget.

INTERVIEW

Those were different choirs of angels. They were running and climbing and making garlands, and having such fun, and they were passing through space like nothing. They never touched the ground. If I go to touch them, my fingers touch each other. I don't touch Thomasino, he touches me. I'm afraid to touch him, you go through, and yet there's a body..... I touch Jesus, I feel Jesus. I feel Mary.

Joseph?

I never had the occasion to touch Joseph. My Father I touch and I feel. I feel Him.

Why were the angels there?

Jesus invited them. Oh, they brought me something to drink, I remember. First they put wreaths on Jesus's head and mine. We were sitting by the brook, and Jesus wanted to take it off and throw it in the water. I said: "No, You can't do that. They'll be hurt. You're supposed to be more tender than that. You're supposed to be delicate, to understand, You're God." He said, **"Oh, that's right."** And He left it on His head and He hugged me.

Then they came over with a cup which wasn't a cup, and they had me drink — you know those cups with two handles? Something like that. The drink came from the center of the flower, like the heart of the flower. It was sweeter than sweet, the most delicious drink, nectar. After that I saw so many Heavens. As we went higher, I could see all the different people.

As we were going up, I felt the presence of the Father more and more and I was more and more filled with love. I saw the most beautiful sight I have ever seen. There are no buildings, no houses. There were just beautiful, beautiful plateaus. I knew they were Heavens without it being said. And the people were more beautiful at every level. They were more beautiful as we ascended. They were gorgeous. And yet how could they get more beautiful?!

Then I saw Mary. I was awestruck because my castle was behind her. And I was at the heights. It just blew my mind. I couldn't grasp it. She went like this, "**Come, come to me.**" And she beckoned for me to come, not like a queen, although she had all the majesty of a queen, like a mother. She loves me. And Jesus said to me, "**Go to her.**" When I went, she hugged me so close to her— just so close.

You feel it now?

Yes. It's really beautiful. So close. She loves me. I knew it was Mary's arms around me, but I felt the strongest presence of my Father in that embrace of Mary. I looked over her shoulder and I was just in awe looking over her shoulder at my castle. "But my castle's here! I left it down there." I was stunned. I looked at her as if to say, you brought it up here? She knew my thoughts, and she nodded. She was making me understand it, and she was reassuring me. She smiled. She was approving that my castle was there. She has the most beautiful smile.

Is that where her place is, her plateau?

That's where she was sitting. She was sitting there waiting for me.

On a throne?

Yes, but not on our kind of a throne. A throne but not a throne.

A chair?

A chair but not a chair. If she was sitting on a chair it would fall through the air. She was sitting, but it didn't fall through the air. There was no floor. She said, "**Don't be too long away from me.**" Almost as if she were calling me to come.

32. THE FATHER'S ADVICE
August 4, 1982

The fatigue is a terrible cross. I feel like lying down and never getting up again till You come for me. It's like a monkey on my back, an elephant. No one understands. In love they keep piling up the work. People are an aggravation, frustration.

"**Rest from 12:00 to 2:00 P.M. The work will be there when you get up. Get to bed at 10:30 P.M. — get off your feet.**

"**Cut loose from the people Capi is sending you.**" *[He names four people.]* "**Block them out. Don't let them bother you. You are handling this well. You are using it for the family, for souls. It's a purification. Your** *[mystical]* **wedding band is a cross.**"

"**The Father has many more revelations for you. A great mission lies ahead.....**"

That sounds like an awful lot: **the whole world!.....** Anything You wish..... **Until now,** is that for sure, my Father? **You never revealed so much?** Never, never? (laughs) That makes me feel good..... "**They won't grasp them** *[the revelations]* **now, but they'll grasp them afterwards.**".....

It doesn't bother me, whatever You want. It's hard to believe there is so much more. You've told me so much, it just blows my mind, my Father. I just wonder what more You could possibly tell me..... (laughs) That's my expression, "**You ain't seen nothin' yet, kid.**"..... Thank You, Father.....

Who, Father?..... He's delighted, my Father. He likes to listen to me. I'm so sick of hearing me. I told him that, my Father. He listens, he types, he listens some more. (laughs) I can't stand me..... (laughs) He never tires of listening..... Yes, Father, he loves Your revelations..... He does? **He understands everything.** Well, sometimes I ask him, my Father, and he says he does..... **Through the Spirit he does......** *[The Father asks her to repeat after Him.]* All right.

"**When you die, Child, and come to Me, the Spirit will overshadow him. And things that he doesn't grasp now, he will grasp. He will bring these words forth to My people. He'll bring forth to the world the messages of the Father, the revelations the Father has given to you.**"

Did You tell him that, Father? He will be delighted to hear it. He was overwhelmed with the Spirit coming to me..... **The Spirit will come in a very special way, because he'll need this even more.** I know nothing's by chance..... Yes, I do, I trust him..... Yes, I'm delighted, Father.....

I feel as if I could go right through You, my Father..... You feel so strong and yet so tender..... (laughs) My Father's with me, what can be against me, eh?..... Who?..... Sallust. Oh, I remember, in the Latin book, I remember..... Yes, my Father. I do feel free, I do feel peace..... No, I'm not tired. I rest in Your love.

INTERVIEW

I was asking the Father what of the past He wants me to reveal of your life in a biography.

You know what my Father just said to me? "**Eileen, your past has all been closely and carefully planned by your Father. They will know you by what you bring forth to them.**" Meaning my talks, my love of God, my prophecy.

They won't have to know your past, you mean?

Right. They would think my early life was a phantasy world. Or else they would think I was a special child, and put me on a pedestal and not realize I have the same battles as they have, that I am an ordinary person who they can imitate. They'll know me by my talks. Look at how many people know me at St. John's. They can accept me as I am — not as a wonder kid.

33. The CAREFREENESS WHEN THEY WERE KIDS
August 8, 1982

Yes, I remember well..... Yes, I do find having a spouse a burden, but I love it. We have so much fun..... I remember how You pursued me. Now we are going down memory lane..... Yes, I remember. It was a beautiful kiss, but I rejected it, and pushed You away.....

They won't accept truth. Not even You in the Eucharist.....

I step on so many toes. Take Father this morning..... Silly, You know who I mean. Father Y. There is something about him that disturbs me. He seems so narrow-minded in so many areas. Some priests are not called to the Charismatic movement, and yet are filled with the charismas. What does the Father want from us at St. John's prayer group?..... **Trust the Father.** Yes, but I am wondering what He's up to.....

I'll come as often as You want me to. I need this peace. I wish I could invite them all into this valley..... **It would no longer be peaceful.** For sure You're right again..... **Whenever frustration assails me, I'll turn and flee to my valley. I'll run into the arms of my Beloved, and He will soothe me, and He will love me. His arms will protect me from all men.** I will be delighted to come.

It dries off by itself, doesn't it, Jesus. I don't need a towel. It's the coolest, clearest water I have ever had..... Crystal clear, almost alive, refreshing, strengthening, yes, I feel that.....

INTERVIEW

Jesus told me all the fun we had as kids. I didn't have all this burden of going out and preaching. "**But, Eileen, it is a burden of love. I treated you as a child, then as a suitor. Now you are working for the Father, bringing people to the kingdom.**"

He said, "**I know it is hard, because some are not going to accept the truth.**" The Father said: "**Those who accept the truth** will advance in holiness and virtue, and the others will fall by the wayside. **Don't pull any punches just to make somebody happy, speak the truth.**"

(clapping her hands) Jesus said **get back to the carefreeness we had when we were kids** after doing my work. I should run back to my castle, and not listen to the pros and cons about me. "**Do what you have to do, don't worry about it. The darts go through Me first.**" I hope they don't throw any darts. I don't want Him to get hurt, spilling the blood of the Son of God.

He showed you the mystery of your oneness?

I passed through Him and yet I didn't pass. I lingered within Him.

You've done that before.

Yes, but this was different. I was in Him and He was in me. I said, "How come I can pass within Thee and not through Thee, and yet be with Thee?"

The Father wants me to get the word out, not to seek popularity. He doesn't want anything that is false. Everything must be strictly kosher with the Father. Nothing exaggerated.

You spoke about Father Y?

I have reservations about Father Y. He thinks everybody should be in the Charismatic movement. My Father agrees with me. Not everybody should be in the movement. My pastor has the charismas without being in the Charismatic movement. The Father said about Father Y, "**Eileen, you will have to step on his toes a little, but do it with love.**"

You spoke of not having to dry off?

We washed our faces in the cool water. It was so cool and so delicious. And I didn't have to dry my face. It dried immediately. The water is almost alive, and it was saying, "See what I have done for you." I said, "Jesus, it's alive." He smiled and nodded, as if to say, You are finding out more and more.

Jesus and I washed our faces and then we cupped our hands and drank of the water. It was so delicious. And then the water went whupp, whupp. It rippled, just like saying, "Didn't I do good for you?" Jesus said, **"Here everything responds to love, don't you know that by now?"**

34. THE CELLABEES. ORIGINAL SIN'S EFFECTS FORESEEN
August 11, 1982

No, I don't mind walking, I like walking..... It seems like every time we walk this way, I see something different..... It's the cellabees. I remember them. You told me they would be mine forever..... They're just about the same size. You said they wouldn't grow, they would stay small for me always. Do they mind being small, Jesus?..... Oh, **they know nothing will hurt them. They don't know any different.....** Will she always be with them?..... **There's no separation here.** I keep forgetting all this stuff!.....

Yes, I like to see the way they bow..... It seems like the first time, even though I've been this way before. It's like a new awaken- ' ing each time..... (laughs) Yes, it's hard to believe it's mine...... Well, thank You..... (laughs) They're trailing after me. Will they get lost?..... **Even getting lost comes from original sin.** (laughs) Well, it's hard for me to understand everything. I thought you could get lost up here. There's enough space, for sure..... **They know just where to come and where to go.....**

It does seem funny, there are no fences, no walls, no dividers. It's all so open..... You mean like the wishing tree? I remember that, sure I do. There's so much we don't know about, Jesus. Why can't You teach everybody all this? We'd be better people..... No. You know what really bothers me? I see them bowing before You, the branches practically caressing Your head, almost as if they were human. They acknowledge their Creator. I think of how we chop trees down. We make fires of them..... It's like a massive death.

Look how they acknowledge You. As if their branches are fingers trying to pat Your head. You can feel the love in every sway.

I'd never want to chop a tree down again! I'd be almost afraid it would bleed..... But it's not red blood. We call it sap!...... I remember that. It was a bull frog and a leaf..... They both had life. I remember that experiment..... No, it makes me respect the trees more for sure. Is that what You meant when You said You would teach me by the trees, by the flowers?.....

I wish You could have had this world all the time..... I know. I guess He intended it; I'm sure He did. Jesus, if we knew all these things, we'd be better people, don't You think?..... We wouldn't? **Because of original sin hanging over us.** You mean if You revealed this to every one, we wouldn't be better people?..... Original sin does a job on us, doesn't it? We don't even realize it!.....

I cut the roses and put them in the vase in the prayer room, and they make You happy, don't they?..... In two or three days? Well, they wither and die..... Why of course I feel sad. I wish they could last and be before You all the time. I try to preserve the petals..... The real beauty is gone..... What has that got to do with sin?..... **It touched there.**

I never thought of the flowers dying in the vase!..... **They don't die here, they're forever beautiful.**..... And You don't think we would grasp it?..... We just couldn't, right? But how come I grasp it? Can't they grasp it, they're smarter than I am!..... **Grace does that.**...... Well, (laughs) I thank You and my Father for the grace, allowing me to understand. So if You revealed it to them they wouldn't understand it, right? Couldn't You give them the grace to understand it?..... **It wouldn't always be accepted.** Why?..... **Because of original sin.** That really did a job on us, didn't it, huh?

You know, Jesus, we just say it put a mark on our soul. We don't understand what damage it really did. It touched everything..... Yes, they were fighting in the bird bath today. That nasty old blackbird almost killed the sparrow..... Original sin. I feel awful sad about that. The Father made each of them so beautiful, and to see them fighting. Humans are fighting too. It must make Him feel awfully sad, Jesus..... Yes, I feel really bad for Father, He made everything so beautiful, didn't He?.....

But did Adam and Eve know exactly what would happen, everything? Did they understand, Jesus?..... **They had the knowledge of it.** But everything, everything, everything? How could they know everything?..... **It passed before them. And that was a special grace from the Father, they knew everything would be touched by it.** I mean the flowers, the birds, the people, everything?..... **The seasons, storms, and it all passed before them. Like a movie. But still they gave in. Yes, the power of Capi. He controlled their minds through greed. They wanted to be like the Father.** But I didn't realize they knew *all* the consequences. I thought they knew the consequences, but I didn't think they knew everything.....

They knew as much as God wanted them to know. And they thought it wasn't enough..... I understand it more clearly..... That's right, **they didn't know sin until they sinned.** So not knowing sin, they were open to it. I think I've got it straight.

You know, You're really smart!..... How do You know all this stuff, if You weren't even born yet?..... Right, I know **You're in the Father.....** It's very beautiful, but it's hard for us to grasp, Jesus, am I really grasping it?..... Thank You.....

No, it's not too much. I'm glad You're telling me. I don't think I could give it out so easily. But I'm glad You're telling me. I like to know these things. You know, I would never get it from a book..... **It's not in a book.** (laughs).....

Right! You're a good teacher..... I'll never cut a tree down, You bet Your boots..... You don't have any boots! Well, bet Your robe or anything You want, but I'll never cut one down..... I'll take good care of the ones I have. Sure..... Yes, I just wish You could tell the people all these things..... I know You said it wouldn't make a difference. It makes a difference to me, Jesus.....

I get excited about coming here, and I want to tell everybody, and I know I can't. They'd think I was cuckoo..... I don't think I'll ever forget the teaching now. It'll stay with me..... If I do, You'll refresh my mind, won't You?.....

Well, He said He was going to use me a lot, but I think it's in this movement, Jesus. I just hate to call it a movement..... That sounds like something outside the Church..... Well, He'll do whatever He wishes...... Yes, I'll be docile..... I'm sure He'll give me the health to do it.....

I'll be quiet there, I don't know what I'll learn..... Notes? Sure I can take notes, Jesus. What kind of notes?..... Not from the Conference? *[The New England Charismatic Conference to be held in Providence, R.I., August 13-15.]* From my Father?.....From both of You. I will take notes..... Yes, I'll give them to him when I come back, I promise You I will..... **They'll help me when I go through the doors the Father opens.** You mean the Father's going to teach me and You're going to teach me while I'm at the Conference, and it will help me? To do what?..... **To identify myself more deeply with my Church.....**

Yes, I guess we do need it. We're losing our identity, Jesus..... Well, what is the Father going to do about it?..... But how will He chastise us? Don't You forget that covenant now!..... Within ourselves? How can He chastise us within ourselves?..... Yes, I think I understand..... Right..... That should stir up something..... Sure I trust You..... (laughs) I see Him!

Do I look radiant, my Father?..... Nothing special. Why, yes. (laughs) "Nothing special!" I'm downing Your teaching, Jesus! Jesus was telling me about Adam and Eve..... Father! What do You mean, what was He telling me? You're God, You know everything. You pull that on me all the time, my Father. You just want me to tell You!

He told me that Adam and Eve knew all the consequences of their sin..... He said because they were innocent, they knew what would happen..... Well, Father, I think I understand. They were pure and without the stain of sin. And they knew what a disobedience would do to the whole world. In their purity they could see it. So when they sinned, everything was touched. But they knew before they sinned how it would affect the whole world, even the plants and the animals, the seasons and storms.

It is a little hard, my Father, but I think I have it. As grace works, I'll understand it more..... That's super. I was telling Jesus that if You tell the people this they will be better people. But Jesus said, **No, they won't be better people. No matter how much they know, original sin is affecting them and they are rejecting grace.....** So we wouldn't be better people, we'd just be more accountable.....

You two are too smart for me..... Yes, I do understand it..... That's for sure..... Jesus said You're going to teach me during the Conference, Father..... Not from the speakers, from Yourselves. That I must write it down. Yes, I'll do it..... **In this Conference, I'll see more clearly than ever the darkness that has fallen upon the Roman Catholic Church.....**

Father, what good will it do for me to see it? What good can I do?..... I know You're with me..... Yes..... Father, I'm getting clobbered now..... No, I don't mind, Father. It's Your grace that helps me for sure..... I think I would have minded it more last year. You're right.....

Any place You ask me to go..... If You want me to write it, I'll write everything You ask me to write..... Yes, I'll show it to him when I come back.....

There has to be a stopping point. My people have gone too far..... You'll never let that happen, Father..... But I thought You never got mad, Father..... **Justice.....** Then it's not really being mad?..... **It's a matter of justice..... It's not the ignorant that are hurting You, it's the intelligent ones that study.....** You mean the theologians, right, Father?..... **If the theologians do not teach what is right, they allow the laity to do wrong. In their knowledge they should put their foot down, and they don't.** Why?..... **Either they are too weak, or they are indifferent.....** That's no excuse is it, my Father?.....

Why do You talk about these things, Father, if they make You feel so sad? I try not to bring You sadness. You bring it up Yourself..... Yes, I know **they have to be spoken about.....** For sure..... **At one time You accepted suffering from me, but now You want me to do something.** I'll do it if You want, if You think I'm strong enough to do it, Father. I'll go through any door You want, if You think I can do it..... Whatever You say, my Father.....

I don't like to talk about Capi..... At the Conference?..... But that's supposed to be a holy gathering, Father..... Yes, Father..... Don't You worry..... All right, Father, promise You won't worry any more..... Yes, I know You love me..... I just don't want You to worry. I know it's a tough job being God..... Don't worry. You see, You know too much. If You didn't know so much, You wouldn't hurt so much. You're God, couldn't You just block stuff out? You can do anything You want.....

That's very beautiful. **You block things out when You come to me in my silence and solitude**..... I love You so much. There's so much I want to do for You, Father. I wish I were a hundred mes, I could do so much for You. And yet, You'd have to put up with a hundred mes. That wouldn't be so good..... Thank You, Father..... Yes, I do adore You, I adore You so deeply, Father, I can't even express it, it's as if it's from the depths of my very being. I so much want people to know You and to love You.....

I do try to reflect You, Father. And if somebody says I do, that's the greatest thing they could do for me..... Yes, my Father. I'll come often, as often as I can. I get so distracted. I'd like to be here all the time..... I promise You, my Father, I will seek solitude to be with You. And I'll comfort You and love You..... That's one way I can help You erase it. Then we'll do it, right?..... Thank You, Father..... I never want to hurt You. I don't want anyone to hurt You, Father..... We belong together, right?..... Forever and ever.

INTERVIEW

The trees bow to Jesus and the branches gently touch His head, patting it. They love Him, and show their love. The flowers and everything show their love to Jesus. I would never chop a tree down after seeing that.

The tree bleeds when it is cut?

It does bleed. The sap is its blood. He reminded me of that experiment on a frog, and it went "ow," "ow," "ow." But when they cut the leaf, it didn't say anything. He said the leaf too was alive.....

It hurt the leaf when it was cut?

Yes, and the sap came out too, it bled. It was not the kind of pain we have. Silent pain. He told me that's the way we are supposed to suffer, in silence. Because didn't the Savior suffer in silence? So the leaf responded more like the Savior. The frog responded more like someone in original sin.

Is that what He meant when He said: You will be taught by the trees and flowers?

Right. When I joined the prayer group I tried to read something out of every book the women gave me. I dreamt all the books started chasing me. They had arms and legs, lips and mouths and they were yelling, "Read me." Jesus appeared in my dream and He put up His hand and when they saw Him, all the books fell into the water and were drowned. And He said: **"I don't want you to read books, Eileen, I'll teach you, I'll teach you from the trees and the plants and the leaves, the brook and the stream. I'll teach you what I want you to know."**

He was doing that before the dream.

Yes. But I thought I could cram in all the knowledge. The people wanted me to be smart. He said they weren't making me smart, they were destroying me.

You said the Father intended this world to be beautiful and at peace?

He created everything beautiful and peaceful. Then original sin wrecked it. This isn't the world He wanted for us.

The cut roses die?

Right. No flowers die in the valley, in the castle.

You cut them?

You can cut them and put them in a vase. They stay alive and beautiful forever, there's no contradiction. If I cut the flowers here and they lived forever in a vase, they'd be contradicting what I did. In the valley it's not a contradiction, everything stays alive. It's beautiful.

The Father was sad about the birds fighting?

Yes. There were two birds in my bird bath this morning. Jesus brought it to my attention. The poor little sparrow wanted to take a bath, and the blackbird was taking a bath, splashing, and having a grand time. He kept pecking at the sparrow and chasing him away. The poor little thing kept moving over, but the blackbird wanted the whole bird bath. And Jesus said, "**See, even the birds have been affected.**"

Jesus told me this before. Jesus said the Father is very just. He wouldn't simply say to Adam and Eve: If you disobey Me the whole world will pay the consequence. He showed them in a flash exactly what was going to happen if they disobeyed. They wanted to be like Him.

Was it a fruit?

Well, you know the theology now says the fruit was a fable. But my Father said, **No, it was truly a fruit.** They thought if they ate of the fruit, they would have the wisdom of God, and Capi was the one who made them believe this. They had wisdom. They had everything they wanted, but they thought they'd be just like God if they ate it. My Father told me that they knew that God was all powerful and that they were powerful, but that there was a limit to their power. Capi was telling them that if they did this they'd be all powerful, there'd be no limit.

So they saw all the consequences?

My Father said all the consequences passed before them, everything. So He gave them an even chance. He didn't just give them a thought.

Capi controlled their mind, they were disobedient?

He didn't have control of them until they sinned, until they disobeyed.

They repented?

They repented, but still they had disobeyed. They were thrown out.

They were thrown out of the garden. The garden was similar to the valley. Everything was beautiful. All the fruit was there.

They didn't need money.

You said, "Do I really grasp it?"

He said, "You grasp it." He explains everything in a simple way, doesn't He? If it were deep, I'd never get it. He has such patience with me.

Making these things known to everyone, giving them the grace to accept it, would make them better people?

He said how many times did my Father in the Old Testament give the people His word, and nothing fazed them right down the line. And He says the same thing with the New Testament, nothing's going to faze them. You have to be open to grace, and He says we humans are rejecting grace.

The theologians?

The theologians. He said they are too weak or too indifferent. That's what's going on. The laity's taking over.

Did He say that the ones rejecting grace were the most intelligent ones?

That's right. He said it's not the ignorant ones that are hurting the Church, it's the intelligent ones. Remember that prophecy, the persecution was going to come from within the Church? My Father said that's where it's coming from, from the theologians. It's not the ignorant people, they're just standing on what they are told.

You said the movement is moving out of the Church?

It seems the Charismatic movement is separating itself from the Church. As if the movement is very special — almost like Fr. Feeney, as if there's no salvation outside the Charismatic movement. [Father Feeney was excommunicated for disobedience in persisting in teaching that there was no salvation outside the Church in a strict sense. He was reconciled to the Church before he died.] If the priests don't get involved, it's almost as if they're not going to be saved. As if there are no good people outside of the Charismatic movement.

You said, "Yes, I'll be docile." So He must have asked you if you'd do everything He wanted you to do?

Right, He did. He always tells me that I haven't studied and gotten into all this theology, but He says, "**When you speak, they'll know it's from Me.**"

He said you should take notes at the Conference?

That's right, He did. He said, "**You're not going to get your wisdom from the Conference, you're going to get it from the Father.**" I can just sit at the desk with a clean notebook and write.

He said you'll see how Capi is working at the Conference?

He said, "**I'll point out to you how he's working among the Charismatic people.**" I know how he works now.

He said you're going to identify yourself more deeply with the Roman Catholic Church?

He said **I'm going to be strong in the Roman Catholic Church. I'm not going to let them push me around and waver.**

You are strong now.

I don't waver for Protestant people, you know. We don't want to hurt their feelings. We're Roman Catholics. You know what Fr. K. said? That when he went to the psychiatric nursing home, the people were yelling and screaming. "But," he said, "the moment I raised that Host, they became quiet, they knew Jesus was there." They knew. And he said, "We can't even see Jesus in people. But they knew Jesus was in that Host." All I could say was "Wow." He's a good priest. He knows. Some theologians are teaching Jesus is only symbolically present in the Eucharist. Fr. K. contradicted that.

You asked what the Father's going to do about the situation and He said He's going to chastise?

Yes, and I said, "You gave us a covenant, remember, and You said, 'No more chastising.' " And He said, "**You will chastise yourselves.**" It's going to come from within us, the chastisement.

He explained how it's going to happen?

He said it's the remorse inside and the emptiness we're going to feel. Know what I figure? That Jesus is going to be withdrawn from us through the theologians. And we're going to start feeling

the emptiness and we're going to be chastised through the emptiness, the shallowness. We're going to find the Church empty,
religion empty.

The tabernacle empty?

Yes, that would be a chastisement. We're going to be hungry
for God. We're going to say, "Where is that Church, that religion
we were brought up in?" We are going to hurt so much that we're
going to start seeking Him, and this is what the Father wants, the
seeking to come from within.

You didn't want the Father to worry and you said He's got a
tough job being God, and if He didn't know so much He wouldn't
worry so much, and being God, He could do anything He wants, so
if He wants to block things out, He can block things out, and you'd
advise Him to do so?

He laughed. He said, "**Now come, Child, do you think that's
going to be the solution?**" I said, "Well, You're God, You can do
anything." He just laughed. He said, "**No, We're going to face this.**"

Didn't He say that when He comes to you He blocks it out?

Yes, He did. Of course I like that.

The Father thought you looked radiant?

Sure. I'm always radiant with my Father. I'm happy when I am
with Him.

NOTE: *In October 1967 Paul VI remarked to Cardinal Leon-
Joseph Suenens that "all our ills today are caused by the theologians."
Nevertheless he instituted the International Theological Commission
which Cardinal Suenens was recommending.* (Memories and Hopes.
Dublin: Veritas, 1992, pg. 183) *The Church needs the work of loyal
theologians who are men of the Church and men of prayer.*

35. DRINKING FROM THE SAME CUP.
THE DIVINE MIND
August 18, 1982

I really don't care to speak. I don't want to talk about this stuff any more..... I know, but don't You think I've talked enough about it?..... No, I'm not sweeping it under the rug. You know all about it, so I don't have to tell You anything..... Yes, I unburdened it this morning. I just want to be here and be quiet and love You. Next to being with the Father, my favorite spot is here hugging and loving You. I love it when You sit here on this rock and I can sit at Your feet. Nothing else matters any more..... Nope, not even her.....

Well, I haven't made up my mind yet, but I've been thinking about it..... I don't like to go *[to the weekly prayer group]*, I've never liked to go. You know that. I don't get anything out of it. I go to help the Father and do what He wants me to do. I don't even get peace out of it..... Well, maybe I'm selfish, but You're always telling me to keep out of places that bring me frustration, so how are You going to get out of this one? It fills me with frustration..... Let's talk about something else.....

Yes, I'll do anything He says..... For sure. You know, Jesus, I don't like to bring her into my communion. I don't like to have her around here. Keep her out and leave her out. We'll talk about other nice things..... Who?..... Yes, I loved her *[Mother Basilea, who was a speaker at the New England Charismatic Conference]*. She knows the Father, right?..... No, I think she has a gold mine, isolated from everybody. Yet, she seems very active. She's running all over..... Yes, I think she's holy.....

See, that's what bugs me, Jesus. When I go to these places I get upset and I don't feel very holy. I'd like to clobber them..... What about You? You told me she looked like a witch. You're just as much to blame as I am. You're the one that put the idea in my head about a witch..... See, she's back in again. Get her out..... No, I don't hate her. You know I don't..... No, I can't see You in her. I never can see You in her. I can't see the Father in her, and I can't love her for that reason. I have to love her because You died for her, but I can't love her because I see You in her. I don't see You in her at all. She's mean, and You're not mean. The Father's not mean. She's a witch..... No, I don't think You'd die for a witch. Maybe she turned into a witch afterwards..... Yes, I pray for her. I don't feel any hatred towards her. You know I don't. But there, we're talking about it again. Let's kick it out again, OK?.....

I want to talk about loving You, and being with You, and finding peace. I need this peace, Jesus..... As often as I can..... Yes, I found You there in spite of all the people and confusion.:.... I don't want to take You into far off places. I want You to take me, then I know it's good stuff..... I love to be here and put my head in your lap and forget everything..... Maybe it doesn't solve all the problems, but it solves mine.....

Yes, I know You love me..... Yes, I know You do..... Well, I hope so..... She's carrying a cup with two handles..... I don't know. It looks like light. It's that stuff that other things here are made of..... Thank you..... I don't know, but it smells good..... Together? That would be almost impossible..... It's super. It's delicious. It's great..... Peace..... No, I don't know what it means..... But we're already united..... **Even deeper drinking from the same cup.....** Somehow I feel as though it has more meaning than that, drinking from the same cup. Jesus, You just didn't bring me here to give me a good drink, You've got something up Your sleeve..... I'm drinking from the same cup, and it's good.....

No, of course it doesn't hurt. How can it hurt? I just swallow it, that's all..... **I will drink from the same cup, and the bitterness will be turned to sweetness, and the pain to joy, the hurting to delight. My love is offering me this cup, and my lips will taste and see the sweetness of my God. There will be pain, there will be sorrow, there will be tears, but the joy will stand forever. I drank of this cup.....** That's neat, Jesus..... Yes, I think I do get it..... That this little one is drinking of the cup. Is the cup Your passion?..... I see. No, I could never reject that, for sure..... Yes, I understand what it means to drink of Your cup.....

Yes, the substance is sinking down..... I don't know. It's sweet, it's refreshing, it's good..... I believe You for sure, but it's hard for me to grasp that I would like anything like that..... **In the days to come I'll remember I'm drinking of His cup. It's been held by the angels, served by the Father. And we drank of this cup together, in** joy, in sorrow, in love, and in peace and unity. This is the bridal cup, it comes from my Spouse to His bride. No one else can lay his or her lips upon this cup, only if it is given to her or him by the bridegroom. Very few and far between do I find men worthy.....

Yes, I grasp Your message. Maybe I don't fully understand it, Jesus, but I think I get it..... Well, yes, I think it's a good thing. It's pretty hard to say. Your grace is there..... Yes, I understand. I'll look beyond the bitterness, and it will be sweet, and it will soothe my soul..... I can't linger at the bitterness..... Yes, I think I know what it means. If something's hurting, or I am persecuted, I have to look beyond this bitterness to the sweetness that sinks into my soul. Right?..... That's neat, Jesus. I'll try to remember it. You've got to help me.....

He knows of this gift? Do You discuss everything with the Father?..... How does that work? Your minds running together, I mean..... I know that, but I see You as two separate people..... Yes, I know You are one, but I see You as two separate people..... Then You don't have to discuss things, **Your minds are the same.** What about the Spirit, do You leave Him out?..... Him too?..... **Three minds as one, but separate.....** I don't mean to look worried or puzzled, but wait awhile. Three minds, right? All separate, yet thinking as one..... Three minds all separate. Jesus's mind, the Spirit's. He has a mind?..... I remember that bit, no arms and no legs. He pulsated. He has a mind..... I know He's a person, a person is a person.....

(laughs) I'm not going to get into that again, but You know me, I've got to know answers..... All right. You have a mind. The Spirit has a mind. The Father has a mind. And they all function separately, but they're one..... The railroad tracks?..... Yes, it's a junction..... Throw a switch? Yes, I understand that..... I understand that, sure..... Put it on the main track..... So You each have Your thoughts, and they all come out on the main track, the Father's. You function separately, but they run together. All the thoughts are the same..... I don't think that was too hard. I get it.....

Then You don't have to discuss with the Father about drinking from the cup. He already knows it. Right?..... And the Spirit knows it. You all think the same thing together. Right?..... What about when You love me? Is that Your mind?..... (laughs) Your heart? Well, is it the Father's heart, too?..... Well, when He loves me, You're loving me through the Father, yet all in separate ways. I understand, I think. You just have to keep pouring more grace into me. That's Your job, my Friend..... Well, I don't know about that. I just know what You teach me, and I'm satisfied with that, for sure.....

He pops in and out like Grand Central Station..... I don't know. I'll ask Him. Father, what are You cupping in Your hand, hiding, yet wanting me to notice?..... Well, I can tell by the way You're eyeing me You want me to look and see what is in that hand..... (laughs) No, my Father..... It's not my birthday..... Can't imagine. Three guesses?..... Tiny animal?..... (laughs) They don't come that tiny..... A witch's broomstick?..... Nope. It wouldn't be too small for her..... I can't guess, Father..... Well..... I don't know. I'm thinking..... A flower?..... Nope. I give up..... What is it, Father?.....

It looks like a heart, and it's not a heart..... Can I touch it?..... A beautiful warmth, Father, a tingling..... I know it's for me, but I don't understand, and yet, why do I feel this joy. I feel a burning inside..... Well, it still looks like a heart, Father, and yet I know it's not a heart. It should be repulsive, and yet, I'm drawn to it, my Father..... I'm putting my ear there..... I don't hear it. Well, not the way my ears hear, Father. But I feel it..... Yes..... Father, tell me what it is.....

At this very moment what do I feel? Peace. A deep, deep burning within my soul, and yet, a freedom..... But what is it, Father?..... Well, I don't know, I know it, but I can't grasp it. I can't define it, my Father..... Yes, Father, I understand. Where do You get such ideas?..... (laughs) I know You're God..... **The burning love of Christ, my Beloved, for in drinking of His cup, I dwell deeper** within Him, and my love is profound for my brothers. And when they make me drink of this cup, I will remember the Father's gift.....

You always stand by me, Father. I know I'm far from perfect, Father, and I need all the help I can get, but You're right here to help me..... I know. I know it's a gift from You. I can't hate anyone, I never could..... Sure, I hate their actions, but even when I tried to hate *[persons]*, I couldn't hate *[them]*..... Thank You, Father..... I'll treasure it forever..... Yes, I know it goes with the cup..... Sure I will, Father..... I will rise above it. I know I will, Father.....

More than anything else in the world. I don't know what time You mean, Father, but I'll remember what You say..... I must not let these things pull me down, ever. There is too much to be done..... Yes, Father..... Forever I will..... No..... Is that the Spirit?..... **No.** It looks like a dove, but I don't know the color..... Will I truly be able to be that free with this gift?..... It just seems too good to be true. I have so many ties, my Father. I do trust You. You know I do..... It's soaring, and soaring higher and higher. That's how my insides feel..... Of course I love You..... Yes, I love Your gift. I love all Your gifts, my Father. They're so different, so unique. They're just what I need, for sure.....

(laughs) I guess so. But that's the best part of being Your kid. I'm the receiver, You're the giver..... I remember that always, Father. I've never doubted Your love, for sure..... When times get real bad, I'll remember the cup. I'll remember the gift. I'll remember the birds soaring above all of it, no ties to earth or man. And I'll be free. Truly free.....

I know it's impossible, Father. That's why You must cut me free..... I know. I feel the weight of it holding me down. But now I'll be free, right?..... I know, Father. I understand..... Until I come to the castle. Will that be the peak of it?..... Yes, Father..... I will do my best, my Father..... I'll remember..... Yes..... Forever and ever..... Thank You, Father.....

No, I won't tell anyone, Father..... Yes, I will tell him *[her director]*. But just him. Right?..... Can't You tell him, Father?..... Now?..... I will, my Father..... **Tell my director that today is a new day of awakening in the spiritual life. Tell him that he will see and hear things that he has never heard or dreamed of hearing. The Father is now beginning to unfold His plan. From the drinking of this cup with the beloved Son to the awakening of a new gift of the deepest love ever, that sets her free from men, and elevates her to the plateau with the Son whose cup she drinks.....**

I'll remember, Father..... No, I don't quite understand, but I'll remember, my Father..... I don't want to go back, I want to stay here and talk with You..... Yes, I'll obey, for sure. But some day I wish You would let me stay forever, and not go back to that world..... How soon, Father?..... Yes, whenever You wish. Each time You leave I feel this human separation so badly, Father. I felt it in communion with Jesus in the morning. The ache is awful, my Father, and it's getting worse. It's beyond all pain. It's like a fire without a fire. Like a pain without a pain. A shallowness. An emptiness. Everything put together, Father. The separation hurts more than ever.....

The chalice. I'll remember. This is part of it, for sure..... If You wish, my Father..... I love You, Father..... More than I've ever loved You before..... I'll remember it's a love that sets me free from all men..... It runs through my soul as an echo that cannot be caught. Going on and on and on. Never stopping. Never resting. On and on. I'm set free. Set free. Set free.

INTERVIEW

So what does it mean you're going on and on and on?

Free. He said it was like an echo going on and on. Nobody can ever catch it. Nobody can ever pull me down again. I'll just keep running and running and running through life, pleasing the Father, not being tied down with a bunch of junk, always forgiving.

An echo of the Father's love?

Yes. Isn't that beautiful?

So Jesus gave you a cup. He and you drank of the cup, and it was very sweet. And that was what set you free?

For a minute I was suffering because that substance was so beautiful, I wanted to touch it. The Father said, "**Don't worry about touching it, just drink.**" And I drank, and it was sweet and soothing and wonderful. He was saying: "**Now see, you're going to have suffering, don't sit and linger on it. Don't try to touch it. When it assails you, don't touch it. Don't let it get to you. Think of the sweetness that's coming from that cup.**"

That's beautiful. The freedom that you have as a result is a new awakening?

See, Jesus drank of this cup. He drank of the cup for sure, a bitter cup. But if He stopped and lingered on it to find the substance of all His suffering, He never would have gone on. I have to keep going on. And this is the love, the burning love the Father gave me. It was a gift.

The burning love was the heart that was given to you. Was it Jesus' heart?

The heart of Jesus.

With the burning love in it?

Yes, it wasn't a substance-heart. it was a gift of the love from His heart, a gift from my Father. I'm not going to linger on any of this stuff any more. I'm set free from it.

And there's a burning love of people? Jesus's burning love of people?

Yes. And I'm going to look beyond what they're doing to me, you know, like those three. They don't mean it, then, who cares? I love them. I'm going to hurt, but I'm going to go beyond that, and I'm not going to linger on it.

You're not going to stop at the hurt.

Yes. And I'm going to love them even more. More. More. More. And they're going to try to catch me, that's like catching an echo. They're never going to catch me to pull me down, because the Father set me free. That was His gift to me, the chalice that Jesus gave me. The cup with the handles.

And the dove was yourself, set free, by this gift, so that you could climb higher and higher?

The dove was going high and it was going down. It was free. It was doing sommersaults. Free. Higher and higher and higher. I'll go higher and higher in my Father's love. Nothing's going to pull me down any more. That was His gift that comes from this beautiful love, it comes from His heart. Right?

And the Father gave you a revelation.

What's that?

Besides the gifts He gave you a revelation. You don't remember it?

No.

You asked Jesus if He had discussed it with the Father.

Oh, I remember. The three different minds in one. He said to me, "**Eileen, I don't have to discuss it with the Father, We're one. We know.**" I said but You are three different persons, and You each have separate minds, except the Spirit. I keep thinking that the Spirit is not a person. *[Eileen knew and taught that the Spirit is the third Person of the Trinity. But He was not a person like the Father and the Son whose faces she could see. She wanted to see Him in a human form in order to know and love Him as she knew and loved the Father and the Son.]* Jesus said: "**But Eileen You saw Him pulsating, and He went inside of you and He showed you all the love He had for you. He has a mind. All our minds run together as one.**" See? Jesus thinks it, the Spirit thinks it, the Father thinks it, but one thought is projected. Do you understand what I'm trying to say?

Well, He explained it like a railroad.

A railroad train. That's right. When the trains are coming down separate tracks, they throw a switch, and they get behind one another and go into the station as one train: the thought of the Father, the Son, and the Holy Spirit.

And so the three of them have separate minds, but they have one mind?

Father knew that I was going to drink of the cup, and Jesus knew I was going to drink of the cup, and the Spirit knew I was going to drink of the cup, so they didn't have to discuss it. Their minds work together, automatically. Isn't that beautiful? Three Persons and one God. Three minds, one mind. They all think the same. That's real love. That's real unity. That's the end of that.

So Jesus and the Father and the Holy Spirit, with one mind, decided to give this child three gifts. She'll drink the cup. She'll have the heart: the burning love. And she'll be free as a dove. You see how much love there is in that?

Aren't They heavenly? They have patience with me. No one else has such patience.

36. STAY CLOSE TO US ON THIS NARROW ROAD
August 24, 1982

"Eileen, there is a narrow road which you must tread. You will be led by the Spirit. The railings on each side of this road are the Father and the Son. We will be your support and strength. Go where the Spirit leads thee and speak truth for the Father. There will be daggers and darts that will pierce your heart and soul, but I will mend your wounds and you will be stronger than ever for the next mission. The road will be filled with stones, with thistles and briars, but I will be there with the Son to help you over them. The Spirit will always be there lighting your path. There will be calls in the night from the right and the left to tear you away from this path. Don't let it happen. Keep your eyes on the Spirit. Stay close to us.

"There will be demons lurking in the bushes and tempting you in many ways, but walk straight and strong, always in the light of the Spirit. The darkness you go through will be the darkness of the Church. It is not an easy task for one such as thee, but in your weakness, you will see My strength. O Child, I love you. The mission is not easy, it will be a difficult task. Along with thy health, it will be a burden. I will be your strength, and the love that you hold for your Father will carry you through. It will deepen, deepen more and more. Go forth, Child, and be not afraid. Walk in the light of the Spirit, and remember I love thee. I am always with thee.

"Thou wilt not go through this path alone. I will kiss your wounds and heal them. I will hold you close so that you will not go to the right or left, even if they beckon thee: Come. I give you this word of courage, of strength. Woe to the man that takes thee from the path or tries to lure thee into the darkness. Woe to those that lurk in the bushes, for I will strike out at them with the wrath of an angry God. Rest in My love, be strong, be sure, be determined, knowing that I love thee, that I am with thee. No man can put asunder what God has planned."

37. ON HAVING A PERSONAL RELATIONSHIP WITH JESUS
August 25, 1982

NOTE: *This communion took place at a Mass said privately directly after a meeting of Eileen with three persons: a friend who wanted to start a movie company, her spiritual director, and another priest.*

No, I'm not tired, Jesus..... I do look for this moment of rest..... Yes, I do like being isolated..... Well, I don't know how rough it was, I learned things, I'm sure. It was an educational day. I think it was good for them to be together..... For me, too. I'm not too much for that, for sure. I like being alone with You. This is my life, that's not my life...... Yes, I did say that, and I will walk in the path You want me to go, but, I like retreating back here with You......

(laughs) Nope. The more I go there *[to the weekly prayer meeting]*, the more I don't like to go. I go because You and the Father want me to go. But I don't care to go. In fact, I'm almost hating it..... Why would it be in His plan for me to feel that way?..... You mean He doesn't want me to get attracted to it? Well, I certainly am not attracted to it. Last night was enough to turn the Father off..... Yes, I understand that. I just want to function in the light of the Spirit..... It's a cross, yeah, it's a cross..... I said I'd give the teaching next week, but I don't know if I really want to. Do You want me to give it? They may not like what I say.....

(laughs) Yes, so what else is new..... Well, if You and the Father say so, all right..... What am I preparing for?..... For Connecticut?..... I hope He does, because I don't have an idea what I'll talk about. He [the charismatic liaison] wants it to be about love, Jesus.....

That's Your opinion. I wish I felt as secure in this as You do..... How can I tell them about that? They must know that I love You. For sure I couldn't go into detail, they wouldn't even buy it from me! Listen You, I'm depending on the Spirit. You better make sure He comes.....

(laughs) See, that's what really gets me. I can't actually tell them how much I love You in the language I want to tell them. And it seems so unfair, Jesus..... Why shouldn't I be able to tell them how I love You, and have them accept it?..... Yes, I know I'm dealing with people and not angels. But they accept human love. They claim they love You in the Eucharist, but they won't accept a loving talk about You..... But I'm restricted. I know I have to watch my P's and Q's. Why can't they accept a real love for the Savior? Why won't we accept a personal relationship with the Savior?.....

Well, You know why, they'd say I'm superspiritual, or I live in a make-believe world. Or if they accept it, then they feel cheated. So there's something wrong with us people, right?..... Well, at least we agree there. But what can we do about it?..... I don't think that amounts to a row of beans, Jesus. We all try to live in faith. It's hard for me to understand that they wouldn't want to have a personal relationship with You, and not just want it, but seek it.

Would You give it to them if they wanted it?..... Well there You are. You're to blame..... I don't know, how many?..... Unbelievable..... But they say they want a personal relationship with You..... **They don't really mean it. It's only words. Clanging cymbals.....** Then you mean when we say it — well when I say "we" I mean "they" — then we really don't want this personal relationship, because we don't work at it..... No, it kind of frightens me.....

Oh, I know You didn't say it to frighten me. We don't really want the things we ask for..... See, that's where my childhood comes in, Jesus, they would say that I've had this relationship since a little girl. They'd either throw rocks at me or they'd say I was specially chosen, I was different. I wouldn't have a chance.....

Yes, I believe there are specially chosen people. I don't know why of all the beautiful people, You had to pick me..... For sure I accept it. I'm delighted with it. But see, they wouldn't look at it this way. You know they wouldn't..... I'll just give whatever the Spirit gives me..... Nope, I won't ever plan it..... Well, I hope so.....

Well, You know who it was, that Protestant nun *[Mother Basilea Schlink, a speaker at the New England Catholic Charismatic Conference.]* I hate to call her that *[a Protestant]*, it's the only way I can pick her out..... Yes, I saw the Father's love in her, and I still think about it, it made a very deep mark on me, more than anything..... Will they really see it in me?..... Sure, that's what I want them to see. I want them to know that I love You and that I love the Father, and all love stems from this love. Without love of You and love of the Father one can't love the human, not with the right kind of love..... Is that the Holy Spirit working? Well that's good. Tell Him to do His best work when I'm there.....

Then You don't want me to refuse it? I think I was refusing it out of stubbornness..... I wasn't? Well what was I doing?..... Was it defiance?..... What, rejection? But they asked me to talk, how come that's rejection?.... Yes, I don't want to speak the second prophecy *[a second prophecy after having given one]*..... I don't — well I do know. I'm afraid one of the women will say, "Look she's speaking again." Is that the real reason I don't want to give the talks, prophesy, call out healings? I don't want to do something else *[after having spoken to the group once]*? But isn't that a good reason, Jesus?..... Yes, but they see it this way..... Sometimes it's a powerful handful. They do an awful lot of damage..... Look how long it takes me to get over that one..... Yes, I remember the chalice. I didn't find it so sweet. I found it bitter..... Well you better show me where the sweetness is coming from because I found it bitter, bitter. I'm not up to the sweetness yet, Jesus.....

Well, I'm guilty of that, I do block it out. What do You want me to do?..... How can I go head first into the situation? **I'm not putting myself forward by talking more than once.....** Is that a solution? If you say so..... Well, I'm serious. I'm in deep thought.

I don't mean to look that way. I just want to grasp everything You want from me. (laughs) I guess I'm thinking of the consequences rather than what You want..... With all my heart. You know that I do. You make me sound like Peter..... Why do You keep on asking me if I love You after giving me something difficult. Do I have to prove my love for You?.....

'Course we're lovers..... You are silly. After all these years..... 'Course I love You..... That makes me feel good. There's an awful lot of people in this world. Yep, I believe it..... I believe that..... Makes me tingle right down to my toes for sure.....

For sure I know You do..... **Even more so than when we were courting.....** See that makes me feel all better..... No, I couldn't even guess, Jesus..... The Father?..... That is beautiful, isn't it? ..... Well, I hope I don't let Him down. I don't want to let Him down, Jesus. I love the Father. Nope, I don't want to let You down either. I love the Son..... (laughs) The Spirit, I love You too. Voice without a voice, heartbeat without a heart. I'm fully aware how He's working in me, and I delight in it, Jesus. More than ever. Since the day He came into me like a cone, it's just different..... Determination, strength, newborness, ever so many things (laughs).....

My Father? O Father (laughs)..... Yes, we called Your name. Yes..... But Father I was aware of Your presence..... **Nobody would notice You.....** That's kind of sad, nobody would notice You, that's sad, isn't it, Jesus?..... You shouldn't be used to it. You never should be used to it, Father. Shame on us.....

Were You happy, Father? I'm glad..... Yes, my Father..... Were You really proud of me? That means so much to me, Father. I'd rather have that than all the diamonds and jewels and everything in the whole world..... Yes, I know I'll be rejected. I don't mind that, Father. Well, maybe I do a little bit. I hurt, You know. That's OK. We'll get through it.....

Bishop who?..... Does he know who I am, my Father? Really? What do You mean, more cautious?..... What is he fully aware of?..... What gifts, Father?..... I guess it is an outstanding gift of prophecy, but he knows it's the Spirit, I haven't earned that, right, Father?..... Then He sees how great the Father works in me, right? He knows of my nothingness. Then he sees You, Father. What bishops?..... For real?..... Yes, I'm pleased, as long as it gives You glory. Whatever gives You glory, Father, I'm pleased with that. Are You happy?..... Yes, You look happy..... **Whenever I reflect You You are happy.....**

An oasis in the desert..... Father, You know just how to speak to me..... If You want me to I will. Which tapes would You like me to give him? I just finished that, my Father. There's nothing on the back of it..... All right, I'll give him that one too..... I don't remember what's on the back of "Spiritual Communion." All right, I'll give it to him too..... What other one..... "The Eucharist." Do I have one on that, Father?..... Right, I'll do that, Father..... "Eucharist," "Charismatic Movement," "Royal Priesthood"..... What's the other one, Father?..... Right, "Spiritual Communion"..... all right..... I'll remember. If I forget, will You remind me?..... Thank You, Father..... Yes, my Father.....

I am tired, Father..... Well, I try to rest, my Father, but something always comes up..... I believe You love me. You're saying that You love me..... Well, I try to grasp it, Father..... It's so hard for me to grasp that You are God and You love me. I hear You say it, I see You, I feel Your love—but it's so hard to grasp—how You could love me..... Yes, I know that You created me, but look what I have done along the line. The earthliness that set in, and still You love me. I keep saying it over and over and I fall asleep saying it, Father, and I wake up saying it, and it blows my mind that You could love me.....

Yes, Father..... It's all that I want..... I just can't wait for that day..... You say that, but You never tell me when. A short time for you could be ages for me, Father..... I do want to come, and then I feel pulled back again. My time of offering will be over, Father. I want to keep doing things for You and yet I want to be with You. It's a tug of war all the time, Father..... Then I will be happy.....

Yes, I'll do my best, Father. **Deep prayer, solitude and silence is where I'll get my nourishment to speak my Father's word. The only time I have upsets is when I mingle with man.** Yes, Father, I understand that well, like the past week, because I mingled with man. **I must only mingle with God my Father. And this can only be done in silence and solitude, love-times with Jesus** [i.e. *her thanksgiving time after Communion]* **and prayer with the Father.** Talks with Jesus and You are prayer, right?..... I love doing that.....

Yes, Father, I'll remember. It's a painful lesson, at least I put my foot down by your grace, and it's over, Father, but I'll love her through prayer. I won't give it another thought, Father. Silence, solitude, love-time with Jesus, prayer, talks with Father, mingle not with man, mingle only with God. Man will pull you down and God will lift you up. Yes, Father, I'll remember, I'll remember, I'll remember. And the angels say Amen, Amen.

INTERVIEW

He said: "**Eileen, listen to Me well: don't mingle with men. See how badly you were hurt last week. Three times in a row. Don't mingle with men. They pull you down. Mingle with God. I'll lift you up.**" Isn't that beautiful? And it's true. When do I get floored, when do I get clobbered? When I'm mingling too much with phone calls, with conversations. People strike out. When I'm with my Father, I'm always high and filled with love and with peace.

You're the spouse of the Spirit in a special way, since He entered you in the form of a cone. So the Spirit has to give you the strength to carry that out.

Right, in each moment. You know He told me why I wanted to reject giving a talk about love of God. First because I talk a lot there *[at the weekly prayer group meeting].* I use the gifts, I call out healings and I speak in tongues. And I said, O God, I don't want to go to the microphone, it's like a display, "There she goes again!"

My Father said, "**What do you care what they say? I'll have the Spirit overshadow you and you will talk about love.**" I said Father, I can't really tell these people how much I love Jesus. They won't accept it from me. If You want them to know how much I love Jesus, give them a personal relationship with Jesus. He said: "**Eileen, they all say they want it, but nobody actually works for it and seeks it out. You have to pay a price for it.**"

I said, Father, if I get up there and I say: I love Jesus with my whole heart and soul... He said: "**Eileen, you're not going to have to say that. Talk about Him and they'll see it in your face.**"

That's beautiful. They'll see the love of Jesus and of the Father in your face.

He said something else: "**You won't have to worry about what you will talk about. The Spirit will arrange it. He'll take care of everything.**" I never forgot Mother Basilea. I knew that she knew the Father. Protestant or not, she knows the Father and she loves Him. At the Conference there were beautiful prophecies, but the deepest thing was the love this woman had for the Father. So it doesn't matter, as long as the Father shows forth the love one has for Him.

He did it through Mother Basilea and He'll do it through you.

I hope so. See we have the wrong idea about love. My Father brought it up to me. The Father said: "**When the charismatic people are wrong, tell them they're wrong. Never mind trying to cover it up with a 'charisma.' You're lying** [*when excusing the wrong*]." And He told me this over and over again. The charismatic people don't tell the truth. They're trying to show the other charismatic people how charismatic they are. They cover it up with a lie. "She really didn't mean it" and "He didn't know what he was doing." And the Father said: "**You're not correcting the person. You're lying and you're giving them a license to go and do it again. Correct them with love, and don't cover it up with a lie. You can't do that. With love you have to correct.**" Sometimes they really want to show the person, Oh, I'm so charismatic, I'm forgiving her. And they're covering it up. And this isn't right, the Father said. You shouldn't volunteer truths to hurt people, that is out of place. But when you see something wrong, it has to be corrected. The Father said, "**You are living a lie if you don't.**"

You asked Him whether He was proud of you, and whether He loves you. Did He say that He loves you more than anybody else?

He said, "**I love you more than anyone on earth.**" And I said, Father, there are a lot of people down here.

What did He say to that?

He threw His head back and laughed. He repeated, "**I love you more than anybody on earth.**"

Why does He love you so much?

I don't know. I'm certainly not worthy of His love.

He said He's proud of you because you said you're a Roman Catholic and you gave sound doctrine and...

Oh yes. He said, "**I was so proud of you when you were gathered together...**"

Just now?

Yes, and you said, "Eileen is a Roman Catholic. She's sound in doctrine and tradition." And He said: "**I was so proud of you. Father was able to say this in all truth. I know it's not going to be an easy lot for you.**"

You're getting clobbered by your own people.

I know, I'll get more so, too. Every time I give a talk someone contradicts me.

You said you would rather be alone with Him, the Father.

Yes. I don't like these prayer meetings. It's getting harder for me. Prayer meetings are not my bag. I don't even want to be with people. I don't want to talk on the phone any more. I don't want any more of this stuff. At first I thought I was wallowing in self pity and that I didn't want to get hurt. But the Father is doing this, because He doesn't want these conversations.

NOTE: *The Father is preparing Eileen for her mission which is to begin soon. He wants her to do the work He is giving her and then to retreat into prayer and solitude, and not exhaust herself with social conversations or talking with or seeing people. He wants her to be free to hear His revelations which she will need for her ministry.*

He will return to this advice repeatedly, and explain its impor- tance and the benefits that will flow from it. He promises her that He will take care of those she prays for.

This is the hardest obedience for Eileen, seeing Jesus as she does in each person, and remembering as she does that He said, "Insofar as you did it to the least of My brothers, you did it to Me." Again and again she reaches out to help individuals, to take the phone, as has been her wont. Repeatedly she renews her resolution to be faithful to the desire of the Father in this regard. As the years go by, she becomes more successful in doing so.

38. THROUGH THE EUCHARIST JESUS LEADS US TO THE FATHER
August 29, 1982

Jesus, as I tried to look beyond the bread and the wine, I understood why they find it difficult. We need deeper faith. I understand my people..... But how can they get it?..... **You give faith for the asking.....** It's hard for them. How can I put it across. I love You, I know You, I see You. I feel, I touch, I love. And yet as I sat there and watched Father God, I sympathized with my people, Jesus..... No, I don't believe there is an excuse, but they should be told to pray for a deeper faith, to pray more.

How can I put it across? I see You. I don't think it's just exercising faith, Jesus. I felt such a sympathy for them. It's hard..... What can I say? I don't know what to say to them..... The old catechism ran through my mind. It looks like bread and it looks like wine. But is it? It's hard for them, Jesus..... But they must know this..... **They must pray for an increase of faith. It has to be strong, or else they're going to weaken at the hour of trial.** How can I help them?.....

But can I put it across that way..... Surely I love You..... I'm understanding more and more where they're at..... Yes..... I need Your help..... No, I don't want to talk down to them, I want to talk with them as a friend, both of us in search of a deeper union with You..... **Remember always I'm talking as a friend, not down to them, rather, with them. Loving them every inch of the way, and together we're going to try to be better.....** Yes..... Is that why

You made me understand it? I imagined it was the Spirit..... Then we're looking at it as an ordinary function, and not the bread of life. Right?.....

Yes, I see how essential these talks are..... No, I feel better, and I'm listening..... I just want this to be so good for You, Jesus. I don't want them to think Eucharist, a piece of bread, a wafer. I want them to know for real it's You. Really You. I need the Spirit's help, Jesus. I want them to sense it in my words. Do You understand what I'm saying, Jesus?.....

Yes, I'll depend on Him..... Who?..... **Doctor Mellifluous** *[St. Bernard].* All right. I will call upon him. Why is he more important than the Spirit?..... **He's not.**..... Yes, I know. He does talk beautifully about Jesus..... **The Spirit gave him the words.** Then he'll give them to me.

I feel better already about it, but it's an important talk..... I'll listen closely, I promise..... I believe that's why we're growing..... Yes, I understand. **If we all make You the center of our prayer meeting, we'll flourish in the wisdom and knowledge of the Father, and that's Your whole purpose on earth.** Is that still Your purpose in the Eucharist? I know Your purpose as You walked the earth was to teach us about the Father, but is that Your whole purpose in the Eucharist?.....

Honest, Jesus, I never realized that..... I knew You wanted to be with us, and to love us, and to comfort us. And You said You would not leave us orphans. But I never realized in the Eucharist You're leading us so deeply to the Father. So if we don't receive the Eucharist, You're not going to lead us to the Father. And once a week isn't enough, right?..... Then we're missing the boat..... Well, I say "we." I hope I'm not missing the boat..... Me? Well, I'd swim so fast until I got hold of the anchor, and You'd drag me along..... I think that is a great revelation. I'm glad, and I will mention it..... I hope they'll see the love, Jesus..... Will they really see it and feel it?.....

I think it's a bad week for me to give the talk..... **Maybe for me, but not for the Spirit.** Then He'll do a good job..... I know. I need help in that area, Jesus. I can't let things pull me down. See, I get to the chalice, but I don't get beyond the bitterness. You have to help me, Jesus..... I didn't think I was hard on myself..... I didn't realize I was doing that.....

I received knowledge and discernment, leave it in the Father's hands. Don't go criticizing myself for bringing it forth *[the knowledge and discernment]*. Is that what I'm doing?..... I guess I am. I wouldn't be capable of recognizing it, if I didn't have the knowledge. So in having the knowledge, I'm being picky with the Spirit? *[by criticizing herself for using the discernment given her by the Spirit]*..... Nope..... I didn't think of it that way..... I guess He's always at work..... Will You help me get over it, Jesus?..... Well, if You say I will. I trust You for sure.....

Yes, I know **the Eucharist is the center of our Catholic faith. It's like the heartbeat.....** Yes, I know **that's why Capi is striking at it,** Jesus. That's why it bothered me so much at the Conference *[because of the presence of non-Catholics, the Eucharist was not celebrated at this Catholic Charismatic Conference]*. It's like he won a victory..... **He did.....** It makes me feel awful, because priests, Catholic priests and bishops, were a part of it..... **But I must not feel that bad.** How can I help it? I hurt for such little things, but that's a big thing.....

Look how much I love You, and yet how much I have to struggle to get to Communion to be with You..... Yes..... Thank You, Jesus. Well, I don't understand You, I know You like my struggle, but I don't like my struggle, I'm ashamed of it. I should be skipping and dancing and running to get to Mass. Instead, I'm dragging and moping and struggling and praying..... (laughs) **These are the petals of the daisy.** I feel like they are the petals of the skunk cabbage..... That's very beautiful..... Oh, I hope so, Jesus. With You beside me. I hope so.....

No, my Father, You're not intruding, we were just going to come to You..... Am I glowing? It's from what Jesus just said, Father..... We were speaking about the talk next Tuesday about the Eucharist, and He told me not to worry about it, that **the love that** we hold for each other will shine forth, and they'll know that I'm in love with the Lord..... That's why I feel so good.....

I know they're filling up, Father..... It is because I love Him, Father. When He talks like that, I can't keep these dopey tears from coming forth..... Thank You, Father..... **You're going to put them in Your box......** It thrills me to death, my Father. It was just so beautiful when He said it..... Yes, my Father. Jesus said He would stand beside me.....

You're not old, Father, You're always the same to me, and I believe You..... That's the only thing that's important..... Thank You, my Father..... Say it again. **She has been daily kissed by the Eucharist.** That's very beautiful. That would make a beautiful tape, my Father..... Yes, I will..... Whatever.

INTERVIEW

Did you have a nice talk with Jesus?

For sure.

Were you in the meadow?

Yes. We were sitting on rocks near the water under our tree.

And stayed there all the time? You weren't there too long today. Maybe twenty-five minutes. Did Jesus tell you what was going to happen in your talk on the Eucharist?

Yes, and He said Dr. Mellifluous was going to be with me and give me the right words and the help that I need.

At the time?

Yes. All during the talk.

And he has words that the Holy Spirit gave him?

Yes. He has beautiful words about the Eucharist.

So that encourages, you?

For sure, because I know that Dr. Mellifluous is unique. He loved the Eucharist, and he had such beautiful things to say about Jesus. I'm not capable of saying them. The Spirit will give them to me, but Dr. Mellifluous is going to be a strength for me.

Jesus is going to be there too? Jesus on your right hand and Dr. Mellifluous on your left?

Nope. Dr. Mellifluous on my right and Jesus behind me.

How will you see Him if He's behind you?

I know when He's there, I feel His warmth. The lover always knows when the beloved is close. There is a warmth there.

How about the Father? Do you see Him anytime you want to see Him?

My Father? Whenever I call Him I see Him.

Any time you call Him you see Him?

He's there. Yes. Sometimes He just talks to me without my seeing Him, but I know He's there because I feel Him. There is a different air about everything when the Father is there. He answers every time I call Him. If I say, Father, make Yourself visible, we've got to have a talk. He makes Himself visible. He says, Here I am, Love.

What about Tuesday night? Will He be there?

Father is always there. I always see my Father.

When you are talking?

Yes. Sometimes I see Him on His throne. Sometimes I see Jesus in the middle aisle, reassuring me that everything is all right. Sometimes Jesus will go like this...meaning speak louder. He wants everyone to hear what I'm saying.

Does Jesus or the Father ever tell you to go to the microphone?

Yes, for parables.

Otherwise They're satisfied for you to sit where you are sitting?

They're happy where I am. They know I don't like to be up there [in front of the prayer group]. But Jesus said the talk is going to be good. He said: "**They are going to know that we are in love, and you are going to reflect this love to them. They'll know that you love Me and I love you.**"

And He said, "**Don't talk down to them, Eileen. Talk with them. This draws them to you.**" You know, talk as a friend to a friend. When you throw big words at them, you are talking over their heads and they feel beneath you. They don't want to feel beneath you. They want to feel part of you. Like, Let's have a talk about Jesus, you and I. Let's talk about Jesus in the Eucharist.

That is what I was thinking when I heard you on a tape.

Really? Jesus says they want to be your friend and your pal. I should say, Let's talk about our lover, let's talk about Him. Not as if I were far above them. I want to be with them, and indicate how much we're going to learn together about Jesus. We're going to be the best prayer group because we're going to work together. We're going to love Him, really love Him. Aren't we going to strive to be better people, you and I? Something like that, Jesus said. You know working together as a team. Not looking down at them. Do you know what He means?

Then there was something at the beginning about faith, that You see Him and talk to Him.

Oh, you know when you were starting to consecrate, I said, Jesus, I see You. I feel You. I didn't earn it. You just reveal Yourself to me, and I'm crazy about You. But if I was just looking at that bread and that wine, that takes an awful lot of faith, Jesus. And this is why they ignore You. They don't mean to. He said: "**But Eileen, they have to be taught. Faith isn't enough, it has to increase. You've got to grow steadily in faith. And you not only have to ask for it, you have to work for it. You've got to be good.**"

So He said that you have to help them to grow in faith?

Right. It's not enough having faith. Nine out of ten of us say, "I believe." But that isn't enough to fall in love. I sat and I watched my Father God. And I sympathized with my people because He doesn't reveal himself to them like He does to me. And He said: "**But faith isn't enough. It's a gift, but it's weak and they have to increase it. That's the justice of God. You've got to pray daily: increase my faith, Lord, increase my faith. All the time, and they have to be taught this.**" He said, "**Nine out of ten people that come to the charismatic meeting don't really believe that is Jesus in the**

Eucharist." They know it by a little bit of faith, but they're not ready to die for it. That's not good. You have to be ready to die for Him.

In time of temptation they will fall away?

Right. But they don't know. They are ignorant of these things, and they have to be told. And we're not telling them the right things. We're telling them about the charismatic gifts of the Spirit. We're not telling them enough about Jesus in the Eucharist.

And to grow in faith, they have to increase their faith. Then they will have a great joy in receiving Him? Then they'll want to stay with Him after Mass for a thanksgiving?

That's right. They are going up to receive Jesus out of habit. Everyone's going so I'm going. Are people going to look at me and say, Why isn't he or she going? So I'm going along with the crowd. I take our Lord in my mouth or in my hands. I sit down and forget about Him. I did my duty. I went. And the Father said, "**This isn't good.**" He said we're going to have to give an account for every communion. Every communion. And that's kind of scary.

Then you said that it was easy for you because you saw Jesus, and they didn't see Him. So you thought you had less faith because you saw Him, whereas they don't see Him and they have to believe.

And my Father said, "**No, Eileen. You are continually asking.**" And I said "Well, look, I see You when I go to Communion and I have to struggle. I should be dancing." He said: "**Eileen, I'm more pleased with your struggle then if you ran to the church. Because I know the effort you're making. I know your faith. You're saying, Increase my faith, Jesus help me, Father, please help me.**" He said He was delighted because all the way to church, I was saying, "Thank You, Father, You're so wonderful to me, You've got me this far. Thank You, Father." He said, "**I'm more happy over that, than if you were dancing all the way.**"

What else did He say?

Jesus said I have so much love for Him, and that we're so in love, they are going to know I'm in love with the Lord. When He said it, I started to cry. It was just before my Father came. My

Father took the tears, and He put the box up, like this, and He put the tears in the box. And He said, "**I have more jewels.**"

Isn't that beautiful.

You know what He did the other day?

What?

I cried over something, and He told me, "**Take a piece of cloth and wipe your face.**" I said, Father, You're so silly. I'll take a piece of paper towel. He said, "**Take a piece of cloth.**" And I wiped them, and He said to give them to you and I forgot.

Then He gave you a revelation?

His whole purpose in the Eucharist is to be with us, right? But in being with us, He's revealing His Father, the mercy, the goodness, the love of His Father, who gives us the Son permanently.

So when we receive Him, we should not only be united with Jesus but we should thank the Father for the gift and turn to Him?

Yes. But see, we haven't been taught this. Jesus knew that in Him we are going to find the Father. Without Jesus, we are going to be lost. We can't find the Father.

And that was His purpose?

That was His whole purpose.

And if you don't receive Him daily, it's harder for you to meet the Father, is that right?

Right. That's right. Did you hear it?

Yes and I believe it. Then the Father came, and you told Him what Jesus had said about the talk?

He said, "**Do I detect tears in those eyes?**" I said, O Father, Jesus talks so sweetly and so lovingly, I can't help them, my Father. He said, "**Well, they're not going to be lost.**" And He took his box and He put the tears in it, and He calls them His jewels, His precious jewels. He's beautiful. Little things mean a lot to Him, and my tears are certainly a little thing, but because I cried for Jesus, they are His jewels. The Church needs a lot of suffering.

The Church is in a lot of pain, so you're suffering for the Church?

Yes, because He says, "**Not by prayer alone are we going to come out of this, we need suffering.**" He cries over the Church. So many naughty things are going on in the Church. I told you about the birth control?

No.

I was at the Charismatic Conference. All those people there, and there are hundreds of other movements going on at the same time, and other Conferences in different parts of the world. My Father said, "**If they only took a stand on birth control or against these abortion clinics!**" We speak out and we blab off in church, but we do nothing about it. So He said, "**We are going to have to give an account of this.**"

What could we do?

Band together.

Some picket the abortion clinics and carry signs saying abortion is murder and if anybody...

That's not enough. He wants us to band together in prayer. We're trying to depend upon man; He wants us to depend upon God.

I see. He wants us to pray?

For sure. Have vigils. Have holy hours.

In other words, there is something so terribly tragic going on, and we're not responding enough in prayer?

We're depending upon ourselves. We should have prayer vigils, and say rosaries to our blessed Mother, holy hours, benediction, adoration. What my Father really loves is the adoration of the Blessed Sacrament. A holy hour with adoration, but done under control, with reverence, without any abuse of our blessed Lord. This is what He wants from us. We depend upon man. We have to pray and pray and pray and depend upon the Father.

NOTE: *Such prayer and rosary vigils are now being held throughout the United States by the* Helpers of God's Precious Infants. *These vigils, started in Brooklyn, NY, have attracted as many as 1,500 people each month to pray with their Bishop, the Most*

Reverend Thomas V. Daily. Bishop Daily said that the evil of abortion has grown so great and pervasive in American society that "only the power of Almighty God can turn it around." (Seminarians for Life International Newsletter, monthly, by Mount St. Mary's Seminary, Vol. IV, No. 3, March 1992.)

"What my Father really loves is adoration of the Blessed Sacrament," said Eileen.

AFTERWORD

The Father wants to accomplish through this book something more than the satisfaction of curiosity. In His initiatives of love and mercy, He is always seeking the one thing that matters to Him: the hearts of His children. To please Him we must allow Him to make us happy as only He can. Hopefully this book will be read and reread in order to draw that fruit from it. It is a companion volume to *EILEEN GEORGE:BEACON OF GOD'S LOVE:HER TEACHING.* One speaks of Heaven, the other of the way to get there. One communicates private revelation, the other public revelation — the sound doctrine of the Church.

This book will be followed, God willing, by one or more volumes relating the dialogues of Eileen with Jesus and the Father from September 1982 to 1987.

The Father's Good News Letter may be obtained without charge from the Meet-The-Father Ministry. Eileen's audiotapes, including audiotapes of conversations reported in this book, are also available at five dollars a tape and a $1.25 shipping and handling charge. Videotapes of Eileen's services are $19.95 plus $2.50 for shipping and handling.

Kindly pray for Eileen that she may faithfully fulfill all the Father asks of her, and also pray for all those who help in manifold ways to transmit the message confided to her by the Father. Be assured that Eileen prays for all who attend her services, hear her tapes or read her books.

INDEX